Theological Perspectives on Church Growth

Harvie M. Conn, Editor

PRESBYTERIAN AND REFORMED PUBLISHING CO.
Phillipsburg, New Jersey

ISBN: 0-87552-150-9

Studies in the World Church and Missions
Harvie M. Conn, Editor

Table of Contents

INTRODUCTION

In 1805, a cobbler who lived to see 26 gospel churches planted in India, and himself translated the Scriptures or parts of them into 34 languages, wrote these words. "We are sure that only those who are ordained to eternal life will believe and that God alone can add to the church such as shall be saved. Nevertheless we cannot but observe with admiration that Paul, the great champion for the glorious doctrines of free and sovereign grace, was the most conspicuous for his personal zeal in the work of persuading men to be reconciled to God."[1]

William Carey's passionate fusion of Calvinism and a concern for church growth was not exceptional in this explosive era of world missions. The theology of the London Missionary Society, erected in 1795, was described as "throughout. . . an evangelicalism with a strong Calvinistic strain."[2] "Rowland Hill was not embarrassing his colleagues when in one of the sermons which marked the formation of the L.M.S. in September, 1795, he acknowledged the commencement of overseas work by Wesley's followers but wished them a better theology."[3] The pattern was no different in the North American continent. As one commentator not fully sympathetic to the situation has written of those early years, "Foreign missions naturally made the greatest appeal in those regions where Calvinist orthodoxy retained its hold most successfully."[4]

The authors of this collection share alike those convictions, and in that spirit have attempted the beginning of a more theological appraisal of

---

[1]Quoted in: Iain Murray, *The Puritan Hope* (London: Banner of Truth Trust, 1971), p. 145.

[2]E. A. Payne, "The Evangelical Revival and the Beginnings of the Modern Missionary Movement," *The Congregational Quarterly*, 1943, 223-236.

[3]Murray, *op. cit.,* p. 148.

[4]Clifton J. Phillips, *Protestant America and the Pagan World, The First Half Century of the American Board of Commissioners For Foreign Missions, 1810-1860* (Cambridge, Mass.: Harvard University Press, 1969), p. 30.

contemporary thought on church growth. They remain convinced that the preaching and application of the theology of sovereign grace will bear fruit in a growing world church. The churches of Korea and Nigeria bear modern witness to its truth.

In that activity, mission theory must be evaluated and authenticated by the Scriptures. Paul, not pragmatics, offers us the touchstone in the development of mission strategy, no less than mission message.

These were some of the convictions that played a part in the calling of a consultation on Reformed Missions and the Theology of Church Growth at Westminster Theological Seminary, Philadelphia, on March 24-26, 1975. Determined to focus not so much on methodology as on underlying presuppositions, the Consultation brought together between fifty and sixty participants to wrestle with the biblical dimensions that must be normative in our understanding of the expansion of the Christian community in the missionary context of the world. The papers in this collection, with the exception of the first chapter, were those presented at that Consultation.

In that process of evaluation, the name and achievements of Dr. Donald McGavran and the School of World Mission at Fuller Theological Seminary have been constantly referred to. That is as it should be. Though the reader will quickly discover many profound areas of disagreement with the theories proposed by Dr. McGavran and his associates, it is our hope also he will be careful to note the appreciations. No one in this volume identifies "church growth" with the personal and institutional expressions associated with the Pasadena agencies.[5] But every chapter in this volume, at the same time, pays tribute to Dr. McGavran's continuous, almost relentless, reminders to all of us that the business of Missions is the planting of the church. We praise God for the gifts He has given in trust to our brother and we rejoice in the way he has warmly shared them with the body of Christ in the world. Our studies, in a real sense, may be called a tribute to Dr. McGavran's contributions.

One should not have to be told, I suppose, that none of the writers in this collection are to be held responsible for anything other than their own contribution. A symposium will always express to greater or lesser degree a measure of disunity. This is particularly so when its subject is the one we

---

[5]John Yoder offers four helpful circles of definition of the concept of church growth in a useful effort to distinguish what has been the concern of the church from the first century from more current theorizations. Cf. Wilber R. Shenk, editor, *The Challenge of Church Growth, A*

have chosen. Very few examinations of a carefully theological sort have yet appeared on this theme in its twentieth century dimensions. We have hope this work will make some small beginnings in this area. It is offered neither as simply reproduction nor manifestly critique. It is first of all an effort to begin to build, on Reformed convictions, a biblical theology of church growth.

We are most grateful for the kind generosity of the den Dulk Foundation which supported the holding of the Consultation and the publication of this book. They have remained most cooperative in the time and preparation that this volume represents. I must also express my personal thanks to Mrs. Jean Clowney who so generously volunteered her time and remarkable talents in helping put the Consultation, and this book, together.

Like all wise men who build, we must now ask if, in all this, we hear the words of Christ. And, if so, we must put them into practice (Matt 7:24).

Harvie M. Conn

CHAPTER ONE

GOD'S PLAN FOR CHURCH GROWTH: AN OVERVIEW
by Harvie M. Conn

Does God want church growth? Is the goal of the church quality, not quantity? Should the church be content with faithfulness in the seed-sowing of proclamation, a "theology of search," or does God expect persuasion, a "theology of harvest"?[1] Are we called to win men or to glorify God? Will an emphasis on church growth not repeat the sin of Israel in numbering and lead us into a new Constantinism?

The first hint of that answer is in God's blessing and functional call to Adam (Gen. 2:3, 27:27ff., 49), "Be fruitful and multiply and replenish the earth, and subdue it; and have dominion" (Gen. 1:28). There is much more here than simply the promotion of "biological church growth."[2] God the Great King blesses Adam, his vassal, with the responsibility of covenant obedience in the world, the arena of covenant response. The earth is to be full of the knowers of God, as the waters cover the sea (Isa. 11:9). Man is called to extend the covenant territory, "the garden of God" (Ezek. 28:13, 31:8-9),[3] to the boundaries of the whole earth.

This calling is not to be constricted to any "Cultural Mandate" in

---

[1]The language is typical of the Church Growth School. Compare: Donald McGavran, *Understanding Church Growth* (Grand Rapids: William B. Eerdmans Publishing Company, 1970), pp. 37 ff.; C. Peter Wagner, *Frontiers in Missionary Strategy* (Chicago: Moody Press, 1971), pp. 124-134. Whether the dichotomy offers a legitimate critique of evangelical, and more specifically Reformed thought, is evaluated by James I. Packer in his chapter in this collection.

[2] McGavran, *ibid.,* p. 88.

[3]Hittite suzerainty covenants form the background for understanding the emphasis of Gen. 2:8-14 on the location of Eden. Covenant law incurred feudal obligations on the vassal who owned property since the property was regarded as the possession of the Great King (cf. Gen. 23:1-20). Adam's dwelling in the "garden of God" placed him under covenant obligations to Jehovah, the Suzerain.

isolation from the "Evangelistic Mandate" of Matthew 28:18-20.[4] The demands of the one covenant of life, now jarred by the disintegrating effects of sin, remain, to be re-integrated by the Lord of the covenant in the grace fleshed out by the redemptive death and resurrection of Christ. Thus Eden, God's "microscopic royal sanctuary, the dwelling place into which he received the God-like earthling to serve as princely gardener and priestly guardian,"[5] becomes an eschatological sign of God's covenant sanctuary, repeated in the tabernacle plan delineated by God (Exod. 25ff., Hebrews 8:5), and the temple design given to David (I Chron. 28:19), and pointing always to the Messianic Son of David who will build the true and eternal house of God (II Sam. 7:11-13), and make the desolate land to "become like the garden of Eden" (Ezek. 36:35).

In the redemptive work of the second Adam, the task of the first Adam will be fulfilled. He "will open the gates of paradise, remove the sword which threatened Adam, and give the saints to eat of the tree of life" (Rev. 2:7).[6] The paradise of Isaiah 35:5ff., will begin to be fulfilled in His words and deeds (Matt. 11:5). In His temptation we will see the One who begins to bring back the garden of God (Mark 1:13), the One who offers in Himself the paradise water of life (Isa. 41:18ff., Zech. 14:8, John 4:10-14, 7:37), the peace between the nations (Isa. 2:4, 9:6, Luke 2:14, 19:42), fellowship with God (Hos. 2:21ff., Jer. 31:31-34, John 17:2-3), the convener of the nations in the new Paradise of God (Rev. 21-22).

God's calling to "multiply" (Gen. 1:28) is not adequately handled by ethicists who either use it merely as an anti-family planning slogan for population explosion or defuse its potency to the time span of an empty planet. It is an expression of God's desire to see the earth crowded with prophets, priests and kings unto God, a desire that shall not be thwarted by the arithmetic of Satan (Gen. 6:1ff.), but will be performed in the covenant

---

[4]Arthur Glasser does this repeatedly. Cf. "Church Growth Theology," *Church Growth Movement. Proceedings, Eleventh Biennial Meeting, Association of Professors of Missions* (Nashville, Tenn.: Association of Professors of Missions, June 12-4, 1972), p. 19; "Salvation Today and the Kingdom," *Crucial Issues in Missions Tomorrow*, ed. by Donald McGavran (Chicago: Moody Press, 1972), pp. 33-36. In the latter essay, Dr. Glasser goes so far as to use this distinction to note the bifurcation between conservative-evangelical and liberal on the alleged dichotomies of individual/social emphases and to suggest the two groups are finally moving towards some sort of harmonization in mutual repentance.

[5]Meredith G. Kline, *The Structure of Biblical Authority* (Grand Rapids: William B. Eerdmans Publishing Company, 1972), p.87.

[6]Joachim Jeremias," παράδεισος *Theological Dictionary of the New Testament*, ed., by Gerhard Friedrich, V (Grand Rapids: William B. Eerdmans Publishing Company, 1967), p.772.

purposes of grace which God Himself will undertake for His Abraham (Gen. 16:10, 17:2), reiterate to Jacob (Gen. 35:11), fulfill in the slave race Israel (Exod. 1:20), and ultimately in the suffering servant and his seed (Jer. 33:22).

In the "crowds" that adorn the teachings of Jesus the gospel writers see a preview of coming fulfillment (Mark 6:2, 10:45). When Luke tells us that "the number of the disciples multiplied in Jerusalem exceedingly" (Acts 6:7), he is thinking of the command to the first Adam fulfilled in the second. Herod will design his anti-church growth campaigns but he will die. "But the word of God grew and multiplied" (Acts 12:24). And one day, "standing before the throne and before the Lamb" we shall see the Genesis design of God in "a great multitude which no man could number" (Rev. 7:9).

It is not "cultural mandate" and "evangelistic mandate." It is covenant mandate given (Gen. 1:28) and fulfilled (Matt. 28:19-20). Men from every part of the world ("teach all nations") are to be restored to the blessings of the demands of the covenant of life — discipleship in all things ("go and make disciples"), call to covenant service ("teaching them to observe"), the administration of God's Lordship in God's grace, the redemptive consecration and enthronement of a people to Himself under covenant law ("do all things whatsoever I have commanded you"). The covenant promise was God Himself (Gen. 17:7, Exod. 6:7). That covenant promise is fulfilled in the coming of Immanuel, repeated by Matthew at the beginning of his gospel (1:23) and its ending (28:20). The first Adam had been called "to fill the earth." In the second Adam, "him that filleth all in all" (Eph. 1:23), that calling would find its consummation (Col. 1:19, 2:9). To know Him is "to be filled with all the fulness of God" (Eph. 3:19).

Even the unfolding record of the narrowing of the blessing of God is a particularism of grace that hints at the expanse of the Lord's vistas. The preservation of Noah from the water ordeal of God becomes the preservation of the world, "a type of the even greater perpetuity of the promise of God's oath of redemption" (Isa. 54:9-10).[7] Even as the three sons of Noah are saved, Genesis reminds us also that "of these was the whole earth overspread" (9:19). The selectiveness of God's now prepares for the universalism of God's later. In Noah's blessing of his son Japheth, this same world perspective surfaces. "God shall enlarge Japheth, and let him dwell in the tents of Shem" (9:27). Vos suggests that "to dwell in the

---

[7]Geerhardus Vos, *Biblical Theology* (Grand Rapids: William B. Eerdmans Publishing Company, 1948), p.66.

tents of some tribe or people is a common way for describing conquest of one tribe by another,"[8] and was fulfilled through the subjugating of Semitic territory by the Greeks and Romans. But this hostile idea of conquest and Japhethites overrunning Semitic lands seems incongruous with the occasion of the prophecy. The concept may have in mind spiritual blessings. So dwelling in the tents of Shem likely means dwelling as guest in the tents of an hospitable host. The idea seems rather that nations being received into the tent of Israel to worship the God of Israel, the ingathering of the Gentiles (Eph. 3:6). As Delitzsch puts it, "We are all Japhethites dwelling in the tents of Shem." This interpretation also seems most fitting in view of the genealogy of nations immediately following in Genesis 10.

The table of nations is more than simply a secular genealogy. It anticipates nations, families, tongues, whose origin does not take place until Chapter 11. Further, in terms of age, the order of treatment is out of place. Shem is "the older brother of Japheth" (10:21), and Ham was the youngest (9:24). Yet, the table deals first with Japheth (2-5), then Ham (6-20) and finally Shem. This is the genealogy of redemption, a list with a backward and a forward perspective.

It looks backward to the flood and to the prophetic blessing of Noah. In terms of the flood, it is an indication of God's faithfulness to His promise in Genesis 9 to fill the earth with a mulititude of the nations. "The world of nations is the result of the peace made with man *after* the flood."[9] But, in relation to Noah's prophecy of Genesis 9:25-27, it is an indication of God's faithfulness to His redemptive promises. The nations are not to be permanently dismissed from covenant blessing. In the fulness of time, God will return these people to the redemptive fold, through the blessing of the particular line of the Shemites in Abraham. "The fulness of the Gentiles" will come in (Rom. 11:25, cf. Gen. 1:28).

It also has a forward thrust, linking the nations also to the curse at Babel and the display of universal judgment. Genesis 11 and the confusion of tongues provides the reason for God's division of the nations. God initiates differentiation in judgment on man's arrogant attempt to correct the divisive impact of sin by unity in man's honor. Yet, at the same time, the very relationship of the history of Babel to both the table of nations and to

---

[8]*Ibid.,* p. 70. Gerhard von Rad (*Genesis,* Philadelphia: Westminster Press, 1961, p. 134) also accepts this term as describing the conquest of one tribe by another, but suggests the Philistines, as coming from Crete. However, Gen. 10:14 classes them as Hamitic.

[9]Johannes Blauw, *The Missionary Nature of the Church* (New York: McGraw Hill, 1962), p. 20.

the covenant promises given to Abraham imply that the judicial act of God at Babel may be a redemptive judgment. God's intervention had an ultimately redemptive purpose for the nations. Out of faithfulness to His earlier promise to Noah, God acted. The sinful development of humanity would not be allowed to reach such a peak that would again demand a world-wide catastrophe like the flood. That development would have reached "stupendous proportions" should the world have remained united.[10] God multiplies by dividing.

In the call of Abraham and the patriarchal period that follows, the emphasis falls on the revelation of the particularism of grace, the isolation of Israel to be "a peculiar people" among men. Blauw has questioned the value of emphasizing this particularism. He feels it arouses misunderstanding and associations with isolationism, separatism, and individualism.[11] However, to neglect this sovereignty of God in election is to neglect a very clear feature of the Old Testament.[12] The divine initiative is at the heart of Abraham's calling. "Now the Lord had said ... I will make ...I will bless ... I will bless" (Gen. 12:1-3). There was nothing in the Terathites to commend them to God. They were idol worshippers (Joshua 24:2; cf. also Gen. 31:19, 35:2), more particularly the moon god, Sin. From such a group, God chooses Abram and manifests His sovereignty in gracious choice.

This same focus appears in the Lord's keeping Abraham childless until

---

[10]Vos, op. cit., p. 72.

[11]Blauw, op. cit., p.24. Certainly it has aroused misunderstanding among contemporary students of Missions. George Peters, for example, in a work which otherwise studiously avoids engaging in any conflict or polemic with modern mission theory, repeatedly judges Calvinism for views of election, predestination and limited atonement which, he says, "would have bewildered Paul," "tragic importations from philosophy rather than Pauline exegesis" (A Biblical Theology of Missions [Chicago: Moody Press, 1972], p. 148). He insists that what he calls "biblical universalism" "holds that God's promise and provision of salvation includes all mankind and not just an 'elect remnant' " (p. 20, cf. p. 69). His treatment of the calling of Abraham concentrates exclusively on what Vos would call "the revelation of the universalism of grace" (p. 110).

[12]By the way of sharp contrast with Peters, Arthur Glasser draws attention insistently to God's "election of Abraham" (Church Growth Movement, p. 20), even arguing that the Church Growth School "has taken this profound truth of God's sovereignty and translated it into a dynamic missionary axiom: 'Concentrate on the responsive elements of society' " ("Putting Theology to Work," Theology News and Notes, Vol. XVI, No. 2 [June, 1972], 16). The legitimacy of transferring election as the predetermined purpose of God by analogy to winnable people as a postulate of human methodology is as highly questionable to this author as Rowley's transferring election as position to election as service (though by no means would we say that Glasser thereby abandons election as Rowley does). We are also deeply puzzled by Glasser's comments that 'the Church Growth Movement has drawn missionaries and national

an age when he was as good as dead, to manifest divine omnipotence (Gen. 21:1-7, Rom. 4:19-21, Heb. 11:11). So too, in the election of Jacob over Esau, the absoluteness of the choice is even more apparent. Both Jacob and Esau are born of the same mother and at the same time. And to exclude every thought of natural preference, the younger is preferred to the older (Rom. 9:11-13). To focus on the same sovereignty of grace, Genesis portrays Jacob as less likeable than Esau, "he who takes by the heel or supplants." "Divine grace is not the reward for, but the source of noble traits. Grace overcoming human sin and transforming human nature is the keynote of the revelation here."[13]

H. H. Rowley supposes that God chose Israel because Israel was most fit for the task.[14] Israel's service is solely "election for service." "When the service is withheld the election loses its meaning and therefore fails."[15] Blauw says there is "no specific basis present in the Old Testament itself for this declaration" and yet he also contends "Israel is not so much the object of divine election as subject in the service asked for by God on the ground of election....There is not service *through* election but rather election *because* of service."[16] These opinions badly twist the very nature of election. In election, the divine saving grace is always the differentiating principle. Election cannot emphasize the gratuitous character of grace if its whole purpose is summarized exclusively in terms of service by man.

---

church leaders whose commitment to historic biblical Christianity has delivered them from the rationalistic Calvinism which is rigidly double predestinarian....Indeed, we feel we have leaped over the inscrutable mystery that down through the years has provoked endless theological debate and ecclesiastical division..." *(ibid.)*. Whether Glasser's insistence on election as a "postulate of church growth theology" is truly representative of the whole school is questioned by others, beside myself. Cf. Wilbert R. Shenk, ed., *The Challenge of Church Growth, A Symposium* (Elkhart, In.: Institute of Mennonite Studies, 1973), pp. 21-22, 28-29, 38-39. And whether his view does justice to the classic views of, for example, the Westminster Confession of Faith is problematic in view of his ambiguous remarks which we have quoted.
[13]Vos, *op. cit.,* p. 108.
[14]H. H. Rowley, *The Biblical Doctrine of Election,* 3rd ed. (Chicago: A. R. Allenson, 1952), pp. 65ff.
[15]*Ibid.,* p.52.
[16]Blauw, *op. cit.,* pp. 22,23. It seems an unfortunate omission in the otherwise excellent work of Richard R. DeRidder that he does not offer any critique of Rowley or Blauw on this point *(The Dispersion of the People of God* [Kampen: J. H. Kok, 1971], pp. 30-36).

In this election of Abraham is also the revelation of the universalism of grace. It is "not personal favoritism of a particularistic god to establish a local religion in practice and design,"[17] but the beginning of the restoration of the lost unity of mankind, of broken fellowship with God. The separation between Israel and the world is a temporary one.

This is seen in the promise of the Abrahamic covenant, "In you shall all the families of the earth be blessed" (Gen. 12:3). The separation of Abraham was a particularistic means toward a universalistic end, the coming universal growth of the people of God (Gal. 3:8, Acts 3:25). "Abraham is the father of us all" (Rom. 4:16). As Martin-Achard puts it, "Abraham is chosen, not just for his own glory, the good fortune of his descendents, or the misery of his enemies; rather, with him Jahweh begins a new chapter in the history of man. Abraham is the instrument for the redemption of the world."[18] The curse upon mankind at Babel becomes the blessing through Abraham. "The God who dispersed mankind by the confusion of language now commits himself to gather them again into an elect community through the Gospel of the promise."[19]

The lives of the patriarchs become a record of the partial fulfillment of this promise. Israel is a witness to the Gentiles of the favor of God on their lives. Abimelech recognizes, concerning Abraham, "God is with you in all that you do" (21:22). The sons of Heth acknowledge him "as a mighty prince among us; bury your dead in the choicest of our graves; none of us will refuse you..."(23:6). Revelation is mediated to the Gentiles through the Israelites. Joseph interprets the dreams of Pharoah and Egypt is saved. Blessings come to the nations through the fathers of Israel. Abraham's victory over the five kings brings triumph to the four Gentile rulers (Gen. 14). For the sake of ten righteous people in Sodom, the Lord is willing to stay his hand from judgment (Gen. 18). The house of Potiphar is blessed by Joseph's presence (39:5).

Nevertheless, these events remain tokens, indications that the promise has only been partially fulfilled and that there is a greater, an eschatological consummation still to be seen. So the Lord strikes Pharoah's house with great plagues because he takes Sarah from Abraham (12:17). Abimelech, king of Gerar, takes Sarah and "the Lord closes fast the wombs of all the household" (20:18). Isaac digs well after well and the ownership is

---

[17]Peters, *op. cit.*, p. 110.
[18]Robert Martin-Achard, *A Light to the Nations* (Edinburgh: Oliver and Boyd, 1962), p. 35.
[19]DeRidder, *op. cit.*, p.23.

contested by neighbors (26:18ff.). All this points to a richer fulfillment, clearly identified by the New Testament as God's justification of the heathen through Christ (Gal. 3:6), the seed of the covenant promise (Gen. 17:7, Gal. 3:16).

In the establishment and subsequent history of the theocracy, this same theme of eschatological world-wide growth is played against the backdrop of particularism. The redemption from Egypt flows from God's remembering his covenant promise of blessing to the nations in Abraham, Isaac and Jacob (Exod. 2:24). Even in the awesome history of the making of a division between Egypt and Israel (Exod. 8:23, 9:4, 11:7) through plagues and the dividing of the waters of the sea, the nations bear witness to the salvation of God (Exod. 7:5). In the face of the plaque of lice, the magicians cry, "This is the finger of God" (Exod. 8:19). Over and over again the Pharoah who cried, "Who is Jehovah?...I know not Jehovah" (Exod. 5:2), pleads under the impact of the signs of God's kingdom, "Entreat Jehovah" (Exod. 8:8, 9:28; 10:17), "bless me also" (12:32). Egypt is spoiled as "Jehovah gave the people favor in the sight of the Egyptians" (12:36). In the hardening of Pharoah's heart God's wider purposes shine. "And the Egyptians shall know that I am Jehovah, when I have gotten me honor upon Pharoah, upon his chariots and upon his horsemen" (14:18). Moses' song of deliverance on the shores of the Red Sea acknowledges the redemption of God as a redemption before the nations. "The peoples have heard, they tremble; pangs have taken hold on the inhabitants of Philistia. Then were the chiefs of Edom dismayed; the mighty men of Moab, trembling taketh hold of them; all the inhabitants of Canaan are melted away" (15:15).

As a regal foreshadowing of the coming of the nations to the Lord, Egypt's capitulation to the Lord is pronounced again in the reign of Solomon, whose "wisdom excelled...all the wisdom of Egypt" (I Kings 4:30), who brings horses and chariots from Egypt, Israel's plunder repeated (I Kings 10:28-29), who builds a house for the Lord as the Israelites years before had built treasure houses for the gods of Egypt. In the prayer of dedication for that house, Solomon harks back time and again to the God "who brought our fathers out of Egypt" (I Kings 8:16, 21, 51, 53). In words reminiscent of Moses' song, Solomon anticipates a universal worship of Jehovah at the temple (I Kings 8:41-43), "that all the peoples of the earth may know that Jehovah, he is God; there is none else" (I Kings 8:60).

That theme of Egypt praising the Lord becomes part also of the panoramic spectacle of the new day of the Messiah which the prophets see as the final Exodus.[20] As the Lord went before the Exodus generation in a pillar of cloud by day and a pillar of fire by night, so in the last day "Jehovah will go before you; and the God of Israel will be your rear guard" (Isa. 52:12). And again, as then, "all the ends of the earth shall see the salvation of our God...so shall he sprinkle many nations" (52:10, 15). In the first Exodus, a great crowd of mixed people had left Egypt with Israel (Exod. 12:38). In the last Exodus, all Egypt shall march with Israel and Jehovah will cry, "Blessed be Egypt my people" (Isa. 19:16-25). "I will add Egypt and Babylon to the nations that acknowledge me" (Ps. 87:4).

None of this was lost to the New Testament writers. What Jehovah says to Pharoah about Israel, "Israel is my first-born son" (Exod. 4:22), is said again from heaven about Jesus (Mark 9:7). As Israel went down to Egypt and was brought up again, so Matthew records the journey of Jesus the child to Egypt and back. Out of Egypt God must call his son (Hos. 11:1; Matt. 2:15). Jesus leaves the mount of transfiguration, his face set towards Jerusalem and the cross, his "exodus" (Luke 9:31). And in that exodus He takes with him a people, fashioned into a people by His act of redemption (I Pet. 1:19), "baptized into Christ" as Israel, passing through the sea, had been "baptized into Moses" (I Cor. 10:2), the new Israel with water from the rock to refresh them in their wilderness wandering (I Cor. 10:3).

Israel's theocratic responsibilities involve the nations. Her constitution as a covenant people at Sinai is couched in Jehovah's right of possession over the world. "All the earth is mine" (Exod. 19:5) is the preface to the instituting words, "Ye shall be to me a kingdom of priests" (19.6). In the words of Blauw, "This does not mean that Israel shall be a people that is made up entirely of priests, but that Israel shall fulfill a priestly role as a people in the midst of the nations. She is to represent God in the world of nations. What priests are for a people Israel as a people is for the world."[21]

Throughout the history of Israel, her covenant responsibility before the nations is repeated. In covenant, Jehovah, the Great King, had committed himself "to help protect his vassal in time of attack."[22] He had promised at Sinai victory over all those who would threaten his vassal, Israel (Exod. 23:22-23). The vassal in turn must promise absolute fidelity to the Suzerain, and not enter into any covenant which would constitute revolt against his

---

[20]F. F. Bruce, *This Is That* (Exeter, Devon: The Paternoster Press, 1968), pp.32-39.
[21]Blauw, *op. cit.,* p.24.
[22]Walter Vogels, "Covenant and Universalism," *Zeitschrift fur Missionswissenschaft und Religionswissenschaft,* Vol. 57, Part 1 (January, 1973), p. 28.

Lord. Israel must hold itself aloof from the tribes of the land and must utterly drive them out (Exod. 23:24, 34:14-17). "Israel must oppose all those who might be a source of danger for her faithfulness to her Suzerain."[23]

In this same covenant context, the nations in and around the promised land become the witnesses of the covenant. In the Hittite treaties, the gods of the two partners were summoned as witnesses. In the Scriptures, it is the nations who witness the benefits Jehovah gives to his people. Hence the phrases, "in the sight of the nations" (Lev. 26:45, cf. Ezek. 5:8, 14, 16:4), "in the sight of Pharoah" (Exod. 7:20, 9:8), become covenant testimonies. Jehovah's purpose in this is grace to the nations, that they also "will know that I am Jehovah" (Ezek. 36:23, 36).

Throughout the history of Israel, this covenant awareness is repeated. Israel is deeply conscious that God is using her history to deal with the whole world. Rahab speaks for Jericho when she says, "We have heard how Jehovah dried up the water of the Red Sea before you, when ye came out of Egypt; and what ye did unto the two kings of the Amorites, that were beyond the Jordan, unto Sihon and Og, whom ye utterly destroyed...for Jehovah your God, he is God in heaven above and on earth beneath" (Joshua 2:10-11). After Israel's defeat at Ai, Joshua concludes the nations will cut off Israel and adds, "And what wilt thou do unto thy great name?" (Joshua 7:9). Israel's history becomes sprinkled with living testimonies of God's covenant mercy toward the nations. Ruth, the Moabitish widow, accepts Jehovah as her God (Ruth 1:16). Ittai, the Philistine servant of David, does not leave the household of faith even though the king flees Absalom's rebellion in Jerusalem (II Sam 15:19-22). Elijah performs miracles, not for the widows of Israel but of Sidon (I Kings 17:8-24). Elisha cures, not an Israelite's leprosy, but a Syrian (cf. Luke 4:25-28). All these become tokens of God's implicit promises of a people garnered from the harvest fields of the world.

In this history, Jerusalem's establishment as the city of the Great King is painted in terms of the gathering place of the nations. From the very moment when David captures the city from the Jebusites (II Sam. 5:6-10), it represents concretely the unity of the people of God. Its very appointment marks David's accession to reign over all the tribes, not merely Judah. And the record hints even at this juncture that this unity may include more than merely twelve tribes. "Hiram, king of Tyre, sent

---

[23]*Ibid.*

messengers to David with cedar trees and carpenters and stone masons; and they built a house for David" (II Sam. 5:11). Already the nations, in Hiram, begin their gathering together at Jerusalem.

It is this association of Jerusalem with peace and unity that prevents David from building the temple in the city (I Chron. 22:8, 28:3). Here too, this prevention of David from building a house of peace is covenant prevention. The Lord, in this context, promises to build David a covenant house, in keeping with His covenant promises. "He shall build a house for my name, and he shall be my son and I shall be his father" (I Chron. 22:10). For the same reasons, Jeroboam must erect shrines at Bethel and Dan after the division of the tribes. He fears the reunification of the tribes if Jerusalem continues to be used as the cultic center (I Kings 12:26-30).

This reflection on Jerusalem as the gathering place of covenant peace and unity is particularly strong in the Psalms of David. The goodness of brethren dwelling together in unity is "like the dew of Hermon, coming down upon the mountains of Zion" (Ps. 133:3). The Psalm of Jerusalem's restoration (Ps. 147) deeply links the city with covenant peace. "The Lord builds up Jerusalem; He gathers the outcasts of Israel....Praise the Lord, O Jerusalem....He has blessed your sons within you. He makes peace in your borders;..." (Ps. 147:2, 12-14).

And this peace will include also the nations. Mount Zion is acclaimed as "the joy of the whole earth" (Ps. 48:2; cf. 68:31, 86:9, 137:1, 2, 5, 6; Ezek. 5:5). "This is Jerusalem; I have set her in the center of the nations, with countries round about her" (Isa. 60:3). "Nations shall come to your light and kings to the brightness of your rising" (cf. I Kings 8:41-43; Isa. 2:2-4; John 12:32; Rev. 14).

It is this period also that provides the backdrop for the prophets' description of the coming day of the Lord as a day of great church growth. Israel's constant failures to keep her covenant oath of vassal fidelity is also witnessed by the nations. Her religious distinctiveness is marred by the idolatry of the golden calf. And Moses fears God's wrath against His people. His withdrawal will mean God's fame will not be seen among the nations (Exod. 33:3, 16, 17). Her ethical distinctiveness begins to fail in the sexual evils that occur at Baal-Peor (Num. 25:1-3) among the daughters of Moab. And it reaches its climax in the degradation of Solomon's moral collapse. And again it is particularly grievous with Solomon since his sins of idolatry and lust are explicitly related to the nations. He seeks to unite the nations to Jerusalem, not by covenant faithfulness, but through alliance and intermarriage. Israel's geographical distinctiveness also fails.

She does not drive out all the nations. And the command "to make no pact with the inhabitants of the land" (Exod. 34:14ff.) is broken almost immediately upon entering. Through Gibeonite deceit, Israel must make a non-aggression covenant. And the writer of Joshua 9:15 notes carefully the godless content of this decision. "They did not ask for the counsel of the Lord." It is particularly in the times of the kings when this geographical call to separation is broken by repeated alliances with godless nations.

So, the nations now serve as "Jahweh's instruments for the execution of the curses...of the Covenant."[24] In the Hittite covenants, the gods as witnesses were designated to inflict the curses or bestow the blessings on the vassal. In Israel, it is Jehovah who does it repeatedly in the times of the judges and kings. But He does it through those who were witnesses to the covenant, the nations (Isa. 5:26ff., Hosea 10:10, Amos 6:14). In Israelite law, the witness was the executor of the judgment (Deut. 17:7). According to that same law, the nations as witnesses of Israel's glory and her shame now also become her judges.

But this very commission of the nations to judgment on Israel also bears with it the ultimate promise of blessing to the nations. And so also does the restoration of Israel. "Jahweh who addresses Israel through the true prophets addresses the world through Israel. He is God of the nations."[25]

The message of the prophets is the message of God's reversal. The wages of sin in the garden had been thorns and thistles, instead of the tree of life (Gen. 3:18), the earth bringing forth fruit only after hard labor (Gen. 3:17-19). Israel, planted as a vineyard (Isa. 5:1ff.,) by God Himself, bore only the fruits of her sin, briars and thorns (Isa. 7:23-25, 9:18, 10:17, 27:4, 32:13, 33:12), a tragic repetition of the history in the first garden.

In the coming day of the Lord (Hos. 3:5, Isaiah 2:2-5), God Himself would change that history. "Instead of the thorn shall come up the fir tree; and instead of the briar shall come up the myrtle tree" (Isa. 55:13). The same Lord who broke down the wall of His vineyard (Isa. 5:5-6) and cut down the thickets of the forest with iron (10:33-34) would pour out His Spirit from on high and "then shall the wilderness be fertile land and fertile land become forest. In the wilderness justice will come to live and integrity in the fertile land" (32:15). Israel of the barren womb would sing with joy for her seed "shall possess the nations and make the desolate cities to be inhabited" (54:1-3). "But you, oh mountains of Israel, you will put forth your branches and bear your fruit...you shall be cultivated and sown. And I

---

[24] *Ibid.*, p. 29.
[25] DeRidder, *op. cit.*, p. 56.

will multiply men on you, all the house of Israel, all of it; and the cities will be inhabited, and the waste places will be rebuilt" (Ezek. 36:8-10; cf. Jer. 31:27ff.). The remnant of Israel, the branch of Jehovah (Isa. 4:2), the two or three berries on the topmost branch (17:6), would produce a harvest, a forest, a green revolution of God (Amos. 9:13ff.).

In this new day of revolutionary growth, God will make Israel and Jerusalem a gathering point to which the peoples of the earth would come. Judah and Israel would at last walk together in Jerusalem (Jer. 3:17-18). And the city census will include also those Gentiles now under the curse of God. Egypt and Assyria will worship the Lord with Israel (Isa. 18:19-24). God will bring Moab, the laughing stock, out of captivity as He brought Israel and "restore the fortunes of Moab in the latter days" (Jer. 48:39, 46, 47). The Philistines "also will be a remnant for our God and be like a clan in Judah" (Zech. 9:7). Sodom, the symbol of a godless world, will be presented to Jerusalem by Jehovah as a daughter (Ezek. 16:53-61). In the coming day of the Lord, God's house would be called a house of prayer for all peoples (Isa. 65:7, Mark 11:17). "It is too light a thing that thou shouldst be my servant to raise up the tribes of Jacob, and to restore the preserved of Israel; I will also give thee a light for the Gentiles, that thou mayest be my salvation unto the end of the earth" (Isa. 49:6). All the ends of the earth will one day look unto him and be saved (Isa. 45:22; cf. Ps. 68:31-32, Zech. 8:23, Micah. 4:1-5, Ezek. 47).

In describing the fruits of this growth, the imagery of the harvest becomes an eschatological theme, the word for the gathering of the remnant by God, the great ending by God of the world's evil history. "It will come about in that day that the Lord will start his threshing from the flowing stream of the Euphrates to the brook of Egypt; and you will be gathered up one by one, O sons of Israel" (Isa. 27:12). God is coming to harvest unto judgment (Joel 3:13-15, Jer. 13:24, 51:33) and unto salvation (Joel 3:18, Amos. 9:13, Hosea. 6:11). In the abundance of the harvest there will be no months long delay between reaping and sowing, planting season and harvesting time. "Behold, days are coming, declares the Lord, when the plowman" preparing the soil for a new seeding "will overtake the reaper, and the treader of grapes him who sows seed; when the mountains will drip sweet wine and all the hills will be dissolved" (Amos. 9:13ff.).

Preeminently the coming of the harvest means the coming of the Lord to visit in wrath (Isa. 10:3, Jer. 46:21) and in redemption (Jer. 12:14-17, 16:19-21). As the treader of grapes, He comes to trample the virgin daughter of Judah in His winepress (Lam. 1:15). From Israel's forest thickets, now a field of tree stumps felled by God's axe, "a shoot springs from the stock of Jesse" (Isa. 11:1), "the root of Jesse" which will grow into a battle ensign drawing the nations to its signal (11:10). The rebuilding of the temple of Jehovah, the reign of perfect peace, divine rule—all the Old Testament promises summed up in the coming of "the man whose name is the Branch: and he shall grow up out of his place" (Zech. 6:12; Jer. 23:5). God will call a nation that Israel does not know; "a nation that knew not thee shall run unto thee, because of Jehovah thy God" (Isa. 55:5). They will gather around the remnant Israel, "a witness to the peoples, a leader and commander to the peoples" (55:4). He will send His army into a new dispersion, the remnant into a new exodus. "I will set a sign among them and will send survivors from them to the nations: Tarshish, Put, Lud, Mashech, Rosh, Tubal and Javan, to the distant coastlands that have neither heard me nor seen my glory. And they will declare my glory among the nations" (Isa. 66:19).

The word of the gospels is the announcement that in Jesus Christ the day of growth and harvest has begun. Zacharias sees in the birth of Jesus the time of God's visitation. "Blessed be the Lord, the God of Israel, for he hath visited and wrought redemption for his people" (Luke 1:68). John the Baptist sees in the ministry of Jesus the ministry of the harvester "whose fan is in his hand, thoroughly to cleanse his threshing floor and to gather the wheat into his garner; but the chaff he will burn up with unquenchable fire" (Luke 3:17). God has come in Christ to lay his axe at the root of the trees (3:9).

There is more than allegory[26] and "basic agricultural principle"[27] to Jesus' use of harvest language in his teaching. It is Jesus' oblique announcement of the beginning of the eschatological harvest day of God in the coming of the Son of Man. "Look at the fields; already they are white, ready for harvest" (John 4:36). God's not yet harvest has become God's now harvest. The interval between sowing and harvesting "in the grain for eternal life" is gone (Amos. 9:13). In the announcement of the coming of the

---

[26]Allegory, isolated from eschatology, seems to be the way this language is used by Alan R. Tippett, in *Church Growth and the Word of God* (Grand Rapids: William B. Eerdmans Publishing Company, 1970), pp. 12ff. So the parables become, not eschatological self-disclosures of Jesus, but sociological conceptualizations of a methodology for seed-planting in responsive soil.

[27]Wagner uses this language in his title *(op. cit.,* pp.40-44), finding in the parables of Jesus his "counsel for missionary strategy." In a complete failure to see the eschatological focus of the teaching of Jesus, grammatico-theological-historical exegesis is abandoned to allegorizing over Church Growth strategy.

kingdom by the disciples "to all the towns and places he himself was to visit" (Luke 10:1), the disciples announce the greatness of the eschatological harvest of God to come (Luke 10:2; cf. Matt. 9:37). Jesus' plea for prayer that "the Lord of the harvest send forth laborers into his harvest" (Luke 10:2) climaxes in a recognition of Himself as the Lord of the harvest. "Go your ways; behold I send..." (10:3). In the coming of Jesus begins the coming of the kingdom, of the eschatological harvest day of the Lord. The disciples, servants of the vineyard owner, are being sent to the husbandmen to obtain the fruit of the vineyard (Luke 20:9ff.).

The agricultural language of the parables thus becomes much more than local color or Jesus' efforts to use the cultural milieu of his listeners in sound pedagogy. It is a conscious use of eschatological metaphor to enrich the declaration of the coming of the kingdom in the coming of its King. The Son of Man has come to sow (Matt. 13:37). And he sows "the word of the kingdom" (Matt. 13:19), "the decisive, messianic word of power that Christ, as the Son of Man, has to say on earth and in which *eo ipso* the kingdom of heaven is revealed and has come."[28]

At the same time, the parables focus also on a new disclosure of God's purposes. The kingdom harvest has come but in a preliminary, veiled character. The Son of Man now sows, but His activity as reaper is to wait till "the end of the world" (Matt. 13:40-41). The abundant harvest anticipated by the prophets must wait while a little leaven leavens the whole lump (Matt. 13:33), till the mustard seed of the kingdom grows into a shrub larger than a tree where all the birds of heaven can nest (13:31-32). The kingdom harvest comes in insignificant beginnings associated with the humiliated Christ. It waits for the unbelievable ending in the exalted Christ.

In this interval, there are obstructions, fruitlessness in the sowing — seed sown along the road, on the rocks, amid the thorns (Matt. 13:18-22). But there is also a germinal power to the seed, thirtyfold, sixtyfold, a hundredfold, which the prophets expected and we may expect also.

It is this interval between beginning of harvest and end of harvest that explains also the classic texts used in alleged support of a concept of *paucitas salvandorum*, of the fewness of the elect.[29] The earthly ministry of

---

[28]Herman Ridderbos, *The Coming of the Kingdom* (Philadelphia: the Presbyterian and Reformed Publishing Company, 1962), p. 344.

[29]A classic supporter of such a concept is Abraham Kuyper, *De Gemeene Gratie*, II (Kampen: J. H. Kok, n.d.), pp. 91-92.

Jesus and His disciples is limited to the Jews (Matt. 10:5, 15:24).[30] And the harvest among them, among those who recognize in Jesus during His earthly lifetime more than simply a carpenter's son, will be small. Against the whole contrast of present and future in the history of redemption and "with His eye on the rejection of the invitation of the Kingdom by the Jews and the sifting out of the unworthy among the Gentiles,...our Lord sums up the results of this history in the words rendered in our English versions, 'For many are called but few chosen'."[31] As Warfield so well indicates, Jesus here is not using the term, "chosen," as a technical theological phrase. He is contrasting the contemptuous and violent rejection of the kingdom by the Jews and the consequent turning to the Gentiles. The "calling" he refers to is the calling activity spoken of in the earlier portion of the parable. It takes more than a simple invitation (call) to enjoy the kingdom. To paraphrase the point, "Many are bidden to the gospel feast, but few accepted" (cf. Matt. 7:13ff., Luke 13:23ff.).

This interval, however, will end. God's wedding feast will be opened to the poor, and maimed and blind and lame, "that my house may be filled" (Luke' 14:23). A centurion's faith elicits Jesus' perspective on that day. "Many shall come from the east and from the west and shall sit down with Abraham and Isaac and Jacob in the kingdom of God" (Matt. 8:11). The focal point of the change will be the death and resurrection of the Lord. "Except a grain of wheat fall into the earth and die, it abideth by itself alone; but if it die, it beareth much fruit" (John 12:24). Jesus, the seed, must be planted in the earth and die to yield the harvest. The beloved son of the Lord of the vineyard must be killed and then the vineyard will be given to others (Luke 20:13, 16). The curse of thorns must be borne on the brow of the King of Kings as a Calvary crown (Matt. 27:29). Jesus' resurrection as the "firstfruits" (I Cor. 15:20, 23), language moving back in time to the Old Testament ritual offering of the first sheaf of barley at the beginning of harvest (Lev. 23:10), also points us forward to that final harvest of them that sleep, and to Jesus' resurrection as the initiating act of that last scene.

---

[30]Both Tippett (op. cit., pp. 29-30) and Wagner (op. cit., pp. 44-45) see this limitation of Jesus' ministry to the Jews as illustrative (Tippett) or purposive (Wagner) of "sound missionary strategy for Jesus' day" in which he "did not send out His disciples to broadcast the seed willy-nilly" but anticipated "winnable peoples." On either view, grave injustice is done to the saving priorities of the history of redemption during Jesus' earthly ministry and afterwards. For a helpful discussion, see DeRidder, op. cit., pp. 146-155.

[31]B. B. Warfield, "Are They Few That Be Saved?," Biblical and Theological Studies (Philadelphia: The Presbyterian and Reformed Publishing Company, 1962), p.344.

In the same spirit, Luke understands the events of Pentecost. On the feast of harvest, when Israel celebrated her future presence in the land promised by God (Exod. 23:16; Lev. 23:16ff.), God sends His Holy Spirit in the baptismal inauguration of the new day of growth (Isa. 32:15) He had promised. The promises of wilderness restoration, of Israel's waste cities rebuilt, now stirring in the minds of the disciples (Acts 1:6) are to find their fulfillment in the new dispersion work of the Spirit (Acts 1:8). The gift of tongues at Pentecost reverses the curse of dispersion through new tongues at Babel and God, through the gift of His Spirit, now begins to build one "fellowship of the Spirit" (II Cor. 13:14; Eph. 4:4-5). A miniature table of nations (Acts 2:8-11) heralds in microcosm the new expansion of the people of God. The Spirit Himself becomes the eschatological sign of the harvest beginning, "the firstfruits" (Rom. 8:23), His coming marks the beginning of the harvest of God in a heavenly land of promise yet to be occupied.[32]

Against this background, two related themes of the Book of Acts receive new dimension. The relationship Luke draws between the once-for-all baptism of the Spirit and the creation of multi-national fellowship in the people of God, Samaritan (Acts 8:14-17), Roman (10:44-46), Gentile (15:14ff.) sealed in one body by the gift of the same Spirit (11:15, 17), announces the fulfillment of those Old Testament prophecies regarding the coming of the enemies of God to the house of the Lord. Those days have come when "ten men shall take hold, out of all the languages of the nations, they shall take hold of the skirt of him that is a Jew, saying, We will go with you, for we have heard that God is with you" (Zech. 8:23).

In similar fashion one must understand the emphasis of Acts on the massive response to the gospel. There is a theological focus behind Luke's recording of "about three thousand souls" converted on Pentecost (Acts 2:41) and "believers...the more added to the Lord, multitudes, both of men and women" (5:14). "The number of the disciples multiplied in Jerusalem exceedingly, and a great company of the priests...obedient to the faith" (6:7), "multitudes" giving heed with one accord in Samaria (8:6), "all that dwelt in Lydda and Sharon" turning to the Lord (9:35), "much people" added unto the Lord in Antioch (11:21, 24), the word of the Lord spreading abroad "throughout all the region" of Antioch of Pisidia (13:44, 49), "of the devout Greeks a great multitude" in Thessalonica "and of the chief women

---

[32]The richness of the relation between Pentecost and the gathering of the harvest is developed in: Harry Boer, *Pentecost and Missions* (Grand Rapids: William B. Eerdmans Publishing Company, 1961). Boer's analysis, however, does not focus specifically on the growth-harvest terminology.

not a few" (17:4) — all these are more than merely figures on God's tote board. They are Luke's historical affirmations of the fulfillment of Daniel's word concerning the kingdom of God. The stone that smote the image is becoming a great mountain, which will fill the whole earth (Dan. 2:35). Between Jerusalem and Rome the great drama seen by the prophets is unfolding. The spiritual world that lay in between them is being literally "turned upside down" by the message of the kingdom come in Christ (Acts 17:6). Jesus has been lifted up from the earth and draws all men unto Himself (John 12:32).

For Paul and Peter, the divine commentators on this history, these universal dimensions of the eschatological harvest are not lost but amplified. The gleaning of Gentile converts by Paul is the gleaning of the firstfruits. Epaenetus is greeted as "a firstfruit of Asia for Christ" (Rom. 16:15; cf James 1:18). We are beholding the end-time coming in of "the fulness of the Gentiles" (Rom. 11:25).

However it is understood in detail, that terminology, "fulness of the Gentiles," has a "predominantly quantitative sense."[33] Shall we take it then as a reference to the Gentile world as a whole at some future date? To say so is to have Paul voicing an expectation without analogy elsewhere in the New Testament. This does not remove the possibility of such an understanding of course, but it reduces its likelihood greatly. More easily defensible is the suggestion of Stek that this is a reference to "the Gospel harvest of the Gentiles from all nations and peoples."[34] It is quite in keeping with Paul's use of the verb "to fill" ($\pi\lambda\eta\rho\dot{o}\omega$) in Rom. 15:19, Col. 1:25 and II Tim. 4:17. In all these instances it is used in connection with the evangelization of the Gentiles, a "fulfilling" of the gospel. This possibility is enriched by the likelihood of Paul's allusion here to Gen. 1:28. In keeping with the parallelism between the first creation and the new creation tied to reconciliation (II Cor. 5:17ff.), Paul sees the universal harvest of the Gentiles as the final setting up of the recreated world by God, what exists in

---

[33]John Stek, *To the Jew First, An Exegetical Examination of a New Testament Theme* (Grand Rapids: Mimeographed privately by the Board of Home Missions, Christian Reformed Church, n.d.), p.229.

[34]*Ibid.,* p. 234.

embryonic form in the church as completed at the eschaton of Jehovah.[35]

At the same time, Paul, as a commentator on the *historia salutis,* enriches the biblical perspectives on the eschatologically quantitative by his concern with how this growth-harvest complex of ideas functions in the experience of the individual believer.[36] He makes no arbitrary distinction between quantity and quality in his harvest theology.[37] Growth becomes a category in Pauline thinking which involves the believer being "filled with the knowledge of his will in all spiritual wisdom and understanding" (Col. 1:9), "bearing fruit in every good work and increasing in the knowledge of God" (Col. 1:10), the body "being supplied and knit together through the joints and bands, increasing with the increase of God" (Col. 2:19). The "one new man," a Pauline category formed against the background of the Genesis 1-3 history, draws to itself the prophetic promises of the enemies of God incorporated into the people of God, Gentiles and Jews reconciled "in one body unto God through the cross" (Eph. 2:15-16). But Paul's description does not end there. He sees that new man as "growing into a holy temple in the Lord" (Eph. 2:21). It is this same quantitative focus expanded by Peter when he urges us to "grow in grace and in the knowledge of our Lord Jesus Christ" (II Peter 3:18).

The consummation point of that quantitative and qualitative growth is still to be. Now God sends men as harvesters of grace. Then He will send angels to reap in wrath (Rev. 14:14-20). During the time of the humiliation of the Son of Man, wheat and tares grow together (Matt. 13:30, 40-41). But in the coming day of the Lord, the Son of Man will put his scythe to the crop which is withered, dried up on the stalk (Joel 1:17, Rev. 14:15).

Then too will occur the consummation of that public vindication of

---

[35]The absence of understanding regarding this cosmic eschatology of the gathering of the nations in the Church Growth writers contributes, we suggest, to their repeated tendency to take this world-wide expectation of growth and apply it regularly to nations and more narrowly to "people movements." Hence, we are called on to expect this kind of "success" in every field of missionary labor. Our contention is that the biblical dimension is on a much wider scale. One senses this frustration with the theory in the response to Church Growth School thinking by missionaries laboring in resistent, Muslim populations. Cf. William D. Bell, "Report on Muslim Work Seminar," *Muslim World Pulse,* Vol. 11, No. 2 (May, 1973), 2-6.

[36]For an analysis of Paul's redemptive-historical hermeneutic in relation to *historia salutis,* see Richard B. Gaffin, Jr., "Paul As Theologian," *The Westminster Theological Journal,* Vol. XXX, No. 2 (May, 1968), 222-232.

[37]Though the Church Growth School is also insistent that no such distinction may be made, their separation of such categories as "perfecting" and "discipling," "Mission" and "church," combine to make such an insistence problematic to this writer.

Christ's harvest rule, mirrored already in Paul's missionary journeys and the taking out of the Gentiles "a people for his name" (Acts 15:12-14), "the offering up of the Gentiles" as harvest fruits (Rom. 15:16). "After these things I saw, and behold, a great multitude, which no man could number, out of every nation and of all tribes and peoples and tongues, standing before the throne and before the Lamb, arrayed in white robes, and palms in their hands; and they cry with a great voice, saying, Salvation unto our God who sitteth on the throne and unto the Lamb" (Rev. 7:9-10). Then the 144,000, "the firstfruits unto God and unto the Lamb" (Rev. 14:4), will be numbered and sealed (Rev. 19:1, 6).

Until that time, "we must work the works of him that sent...while it is day: the night cometh when no man can work" (John 9:4). We plow in hope.

CHAPTER TWO

AN INTRODUCTION TO THE
CHURCH GROWTH PERSPECTIVES
OF
DONALD ANDERSON McGAVRAN

by Arthur F. Glasser*

Introduction

This consultation has been convened to grapple with the theological implications of one of the church's outstanding missiologists, Donald Anderson McGavran. Our task is to listen and learn, to question and to grow in our understanding of the task before us touching the growth of our Reformed churches. Our method will be inquiry. We shall search together—not only to discover where we disagree, but to appreciate where we may disagree. I pray that we shall be free from arrogance, free from the temptation to misrepresent the convictions of others, and free from the criticism that is not wholly motivated by Christian love. May we seek the clarification and elevation of the truth as it is in Jesus Christ.

Where to begin? Dr. McGavran's first book was an analytical study of the growth of the church in Central India and was an immediate success. *Christian Missions in Mid-India* (1936) went through several editions.

Arthur F. Glasser is Dean of the School of World Mission at Fuller Theological Seminary and Associate Professor of Theology, Mission and East Asian Studies. From 1946 to 1951, he served on the Chinese mainland with the China Inland Mission. He returned home to teaching responsibilities at Columbia Bible College and then to administrative responsibilities with the Overseas Missionary Fellowship. He is an ordained minister of the Reformed Presbyterian Church, Evangelical Synod.

Other missiologists (Bishop J. W. Pickett, Rev. A. H. Singh, and Dr. A. L. Warshuis) added chapters. Its present name is *Church Growth and Group Conversion.* Dr. John R. Mott, then President of the International Missionary Council, wrote in the foreword to the 1938 edition:

> The distinctive and important contribution of this most instructive, stimulating and reassuring book has been that of setting forth with clarity and frankness why the work of so many churches and mission stations has been so comparatively sterile, and why in other cases their labors have been attended with wonderful fruitfulness.[1]

Preceding this foreword is Dr. McGavran's dedication. It reads as follows:

> Dedicated to those men and women who labor for the growth of the churches, discarding theories of church growth which do not work and learning and practicing productive patterns which actually disciple the peoples and increase the Household of God.[2]

It seems to me that these two statements might well set the tone for this consultation. The components that were central to Dr. McGavran's concern in 1938 are dominant in his thought today. They are represented by the action verbs in his dedication and by the buoyant mood of Dr. Mott's foreword. Permit this summarization at the outset of our deliberations.

Labor! The work of church growth is not readily accomplished without much thought, much pain, and much prayer.

Discard! All theories of church growth which have not produced results should be cast aside in the desire to be faithful to God.

Learn! Be open to the insights of those whom God has singularly used in many parts of the world to produce church growth.

Practice! Be willing to apply, under God, those patterns of church growth He has already been pleased to use to gather His people to Himself in great numbers.

Theological Heritage

Dr. McGavran's roots are deeply imbedded in the Christian Church-Disciples of Christ, an early 19th century restoration movement that developed simultaneously in Scotland and on the American frontier. Its

---

[1] J. W. Pickett, A. L. Warushuis, G. H. Singh, D. A. McGavran, *Church Growth and Group Conversion* (Lucknow, U.P., India: Lucknow Publishing House, 1962).

[2] *Ibid.*

initial focus was a reaction against all narrow bigotry in the sphere of religion. At its heart was a "passion for the unity of the Body of Christ, an abhorrence of party spirit, and a deep conviction that no unity could be achieved until the life, faith and order of the New Testament Church were restored."[3]

Although its founders (Barton H. Stone, Richard McNemar, Thomas and Alexander Campbell, William Jones and James Wallis) were theologically trained and knowledgeable touching the Reformed faith, they repudiated the thesis that the opinions of men—the creedal affirmations of the Reformers and their successors—should be made tests of Christian fellowship. Indeed, in their judgment these creeds kept Christians apart. Of course, this does not mean that they rejected the doctrines or were hostile toward the attempts of men to systematize biblical truth. Their only concern was that the results should not be made binding upon others. "The exaltation of the Lordship of Jesus Christ above human opinions is the very Magna Carta of our religious liberty."[4] They were "tired and sick of the bitter jarrings and janglings of a party spirit" that characterized the Protestant movement in their day and were determined to take such steps as would "restore unity, peace and purity to the whole church of God."[5] This passion for the expressed and experienced unity of the people of God explains why down through the years Disciples have participated in almost every conference and meeting convened to grapple with the issue of the unity of the church.

Hence when we reflect on Dr. McGavran's theological contribution to the Church Growth movement, we must keep in mind this heritage. He is not sectarian. He is willing to receive all who profess faith in Jesus Christ as God and Savior, regardless of their religious tradition. He refuses to be isolated from any segment of the church. Although an admirer of Dr. J. Gresham Machen for his loyalty to Scripture and his bold confession of the faith once delivered to the saints, Dr. McGavran would question both the scripturalness and the pragmatic advantages to be gained by the separatism that is part of Dr. Machen's legacy to his followers.

Reformation Theology

Dr. McGavran regards some components of Lutheran and Calvinistic

---

[3]William Robinson, *What Churches of Christ Stand For* (Birmingham, England: The Berean Press, 1946), p. 24.

[4]James Harvey Garrison, *Reformation of the Nineteenth Century* (St. Louis, Mo.: Christian Publishing Company, 1901), p. 507.

[5]Campbell's Declaration of 1809.

theology as time-conditioned and polemical. This theology received its original impetus from the felt obligation of the Reformers to challenge the terrible distortions of biblical truth that had developed under the papal system. Dr. McGavran recognizes that the Reformers had to expose as contrary to Scripture the Roman concept that God is reluctant to save men and must be bargained with by man's self-abasement and good works, or by pleading the merit of works of supererogation. As a result of their necessary polemic stance the Reformers were prevented from being able to comprehend the total range of biblical truth. This is not to castigate them, but to underscore the importance of guarding against the temptation of making any time-conditioned human statement of truth normative for later generations of the church. Dr. McGavran enthusiastically endorses the thesis that the church is always under the cross and under the Scriptures. And he admires the Reformers for embracing the cross and binding their consciences to God's holy Word. In his judgment, however, they were so eager to exalt God as the Author of salvation and guard his initiative in the conversion process that their devoted successors easily domesticated great truths and transformed them into an introverted churchism that made the institutional church an end in itself. Much of Dr. McGavran's theologizing focuses on this introverted churchism.

Furthermore, Dr. McGavran sees early Protestantism failing to repudiate the Roman legacy of the subservience of church to state. This brought a provincialism (a *Volk* orientation) to the perspectives of the Reformers on the church in the world. The counterpart of this Volk/Land/Church fusion was that the individual was unable to decide for himself whether to be a Christian. Paedobaptism was unconsciously made the outer and formal sign of the ethnic unity of the visible people of God. According to Yoder the Reformers held that:

> The individual was still free to decide whether truly to believe—and Luther, like his father Augustine, was no optimist about the relative number of true believers—but the question of authentic personal experience and commitment was not to be a precondition for being a member of the visible Christian community, to baptism or communion. Properly, for the sake of its authenticity, true inner decision must be left hidden, a secret between each man and God.[6]

Later, under the pressure of the Anabaptists with their call for conscious decision for Christ and their stress on expressing this decision openly, the

---

[6]Howard J. Yoder, "Reformation and Missions: A Literature Review," *Occasional Bulletin: Missionary Research Library* XXII (June, 1971), p. 5.

Reformed churches began to add to the confirmation process a meaningful, adult, uncoerced profession of faith. This was a mediating step in the direction of a believers-church ecclesiology. However, it must be underscored that the pietistic call for conscious decision was initially made in their *Gemeinschaft* sodality structures that theologians of the Reformed tradition rejected as the resurgence of Medieval monasticism. Nonetheless, it was these sodalities that developed both the theory and the practice of mission — the sending, proclaiming and congregation-planting that ushered in the Protestant missionary movement.

All this is grist for Dr. McGavran's mill. One of the central tasks he assigns students in his *Theology of Missions Today* course is the critical evaluation of the creedal affirmations of their churches. Are they true to Scripture? Do they adequately present the missionary mandate? The introduction to this assignment reads as follows:

Let me sum up very briefly what I shall be saying for several days in many different ways and what you will be working on, each in his own way, for several days. I set before you four propositions:

(1) Most of the current creeds, both written and unwritten, were framed during the centuries when the Protestant churches were sealed off from the non-Christian world and were almost completely non-missionary.

(2) Most doctrines are deficient in the missionary dimension. They were formulated for existing Christians against the errors and mistakes of other Christians. They were not formulated under the impulsion of the Great Commission. This has greatly hindered the spread of the Gospel.

(3) Since the Great Commission is an integral part of the Bible and is a central strand in God's revelation and Christ's atoning death, this also means that many doctrines are not as biblical as they might be.

(4) Christians (theologians, missionaries, ministers and others) do well when they seek to make each doctrine biblically more true and missionarily more adequate. Each doctrine should drive Christians and churches out to the evangelization of the three billion.

The task he then assigns is rather formidable. Each student is pressed to tackle the particular creed of his church and make it more biblical and more missionarily adequate. This exercise is an eye-opener, to say the least. How limited the creeds that came out of the Reformation! It becomes quite apparent from an exercise such as this, that Dr. McGavran has a distinct theological method.

Theological Method

Dr. McGavran's theological method does not involve the orderly unfolding of a system based on inner-evolved principles. He is no system builder, operating according to a particular set of self-selected norms. Where the Scriptures are silent, he desires to remain silent. For example, he would offer no resolution to the paradox of the sovereignty of God and the responsibility of man. Indeed, he would challenge the rightness of attempting to supply this supposed deficiency by a tightly reasoned decretal theology. He would argue that such an attempted solution might encourage the church to rationalize away her sense of obligation to evangelize the nations. He would point out that all too frequently this has happened with the Reformed tradition.

In Dr. McGavran we have a missiologist, not a theologian in the traditional sense. His all-consuming interest is the biblical priority that he describes as "the center" of the church's task. The center is the proclamation of the Gosepl, the gathering of converts into existing congregations, the multiplying of new congregations—in short, the extension of the Christian movement by all available means. As a result, his theologizing is somewhat after the model of G. C. Berkouwer's principle of "co-relationship." Berkouwer contends that theology to be valid should not be developed according to self-selected norms—that is, for its own sake. Smedes summarizes this style as follows:

> Theology is in constant and dynamic relationship with faith and, hence, with the Word of God, on the one hand, and with the Church and the pulpit on the other. Only as it lives and works at the center of this double polarity can theology be meaningful and relevant.[7]

Striking an analogy we might say that in Dr. McGavran's hand and heart is the Word of God. In the forefront of his concern is the empirical church, her congregations scattered throughout a world in which three billion people have yet to hear the Gosepl and be persuaded to repent and believe in Jesus Christ. Dr. McGavran's theologizing keeps the components of Scripture, church and mission in constant and dynamic interaction.

---

[7]Lewis B. Smedes, "G. C. Berkouwer," *Creative Minds in Contemporary Theology,* ed. Philip Edgecumbe Hughes (Grand Rapids, Michigan: William B. Eerdmans Publishing Company, 1973), pp. 63-98.

He never gets far away from the agonizing reality that if this generation is to be evangelized, there must be a fantastic increase in the number of congregations caught up in the missionary purpose of God. He is not interested in producing theological essays unrelated to this task. Nor does he have much patience with those who profess their loyalty to Christ and their submission to Scripture, yet remain only marginally interested in evangelism and missions. He would confront us with the tragically slow growth of the churches of the Reformed tradition in America and then ask us searching questions as to our understanding of "The ministry which (we) have received from the Lord" and the steps that we are taking to "fulfil it" (Col. 4:17). Let me explain.

The Service of Christ (Διακονία)

When the Apostle Paul said that there are "varieties of service (διακονίαι pl.) but the same Lord" (I Cor. 12:5) he included all the forms which the service of Christ may take within the fellowship of the people of God and among the peoples of the world. All spiritual gifts (δομάτα, χαρισμάτα) are for the equipment of the saints, for this work of ministry (διακονία), in which the Body of Christ is built up (Eph. 4:8, 12). According to Scripture the term "ministry" embraces both the specific service of material relief and the total range of Christian duties, whether internally to the believing corpus or externally to the unbelieving world. The whole church is called to this diaconate. When every part of the Body is "working properly" the result is both bodily growth and spiritual upbuilding "in love" (v. 16). It should be noted that Paul's phrase: "building up the body of Christ" (v. 12) uses the same word (οἰκοδομέω) found in our Lord's affirmation: "I will build My Church" (Matt. 16:18). Since Christ's building of the Church involves both conversion growth and perfection growth the ministry of the diaconate is external as well as internal.

The internal διακονία embraces the local congregation's ministry to the Lord in worship by prayer, sacrament and the hearing of the Word of God (Acts 13:2), the ministry of its members to one another "for their common good" (I Cor. 12:7; II Cor. 8:4), and the ministry of teaching by which the believing congregation is inculcated with the norms of the apostolic tradition (Acts 6:4; Rom. 12:7). These three: worship, sharing, and instruction are essential to the vitality of the inner life - the κοινωνία - of the people of God.

The external διακονία likewise has three components. There is the specific calling of the church to minister to those in special need: the poor, the sick, the widow, the orphan, the prisoner, the homeless and the stranger within the gates. Paul clearly states that God sets apart certain men and women for works of mercy and relief (Rom. 12:7; Gal. 6:10a). In addition, there is the ministry of reconciliation whereby Christians work for justice and concord between men and within society as well as for their reconciliation to God through the Gospel (II Cor. 5:18-21). Finally, there is the διακονία of mission. The church has often tended to regard her evangelistic and missionary calling as on a somewhat lower level of importance than her obligation to respond to man's physical and social needs. Dr. McGavran contends that the very life and death of Christ, the very pattern of His witness and service among men, and His mandate for evangelism and missionary expansion are all intimately related to what He would have His people do to minister to the total needs of mankind. As Visser t'Hooft so pointedly summarizes:

> We serve (διακονία) because we are followers of the great Servant. But we know that the supreme service consists in bringing people to the Servant Himself....It is an illusion to think that our service can be made so transparent that it will by itself lead those whom we serve to a confrontation with Jesus Christ.[8]

In summary, the external διακονία embraces the obligation to service, to reconciliation and to mission. When placed alongside the components of internal, the total picture is as follows:

MINISTRY
of the
PEOPLE OF GOD
διακονία

INTERNAL   EXTERNAL
to the Body   through the Body

Worship	Sharing	Teaching	Service	Reconciliational	Mission
(1)	(2)	(3)	(4)	(5)	(6)
λειτουργία	κοινωνία διακονία	διδασκαλία	διακονία	καταλλαγή	μαρτυρία
(spiritual)	(social)	(intellectual)	(physical)	(social)	(spiritual)

We have developed this theme of ministry at some length because of its intimate relation to Dr. McGavran's theological method of "co-relationship." The following specific illustration will bring this into focus.

In a recent issue of the *Reformed Journal* (December, 1974), Dr. Nicholas Wolterstorff described the three major patterns of Christian life and conviction that currently characterize the Christian Reformed Church.[9]

1. *Pietists:* Those who cultivate personal piety and who largely treat the Bible as a devotional book. They avoid culture (insofar as that is possible) and are more or less separate from the rest of society. They have family devotions before and after meals, avoid Sunday work and recreation, attend church twice on Sundays, do not use alcohol, and in other ways cultivate a distinctly Reformed pattern of piety. Their priority is items 1 and 2 on our diagram.

2. *Doctrinalists:* Those who see the appropriate response to the Gospel as consisting primarily in the acceptance of true doctrine. The Bible is the medium by which these true doctrines are transmitted from God to His people. Theology thus becomes an immensely important enterprise. The tenets of the Reformed faith are mastered and they become normative for interpreting Scripture. Their priority is item 3 on our diagram.

3. *Kuyperians:* Those who do not deny genuine piety or true doctrine but who do not feel that the heart of the appropriate response to the gospel consists in these. Rather it is the task of God's people to do His will in all areas of life and seek to reform society in accordance with His laws. They do not avoid culture and society—their task is to reform it. Their priority is items 4 and 5 on our diagram.

But what is the relation of those three responses to Dr. McGavran and the Church Growth movement? It so happens that within the past year Dr. McGavran and his associates have been in extended conversation with the Home Missions staff of the Christian Reformed Church. These discussions have arisen because of the growing awareness of these brethren that their church is in trouble. And the trouble is not that these three responses are unimportant, or that they are devoid of biblical basis. Indeed, who can fault personal piety, doctrinal integrity, and the cultural mandate?

⁸Willem Adolph Visser t'Hooft, *The Pressure of Our Common Calling* (Garden City, N. Y.: Doubleday, 1959), pp. 57, 55.

⁹Nicholas Wolterstorff, "The AACS in the CRC," *Reformed Journal*, Vol. XXIV, December, 1974), p. 10.

¹⁰Donald McGavran, memo, dated February 26, 1974 to his colleagues at the Fuller School of World Mission.

The Christian Reformed Church is in trouble because the average age of its members is increasing, rather than decreasing. It is losing its ability to retain the allegiance of its covenant children. It is not growing. In fact, its leadership is not uniformly convinced that its lack of growth is a deficiency which should be corrected. In a memo addressed to his associates in the School of World Mission, Dr. McGavran wrote:

> The Christian Reformed people have become so indigenous to the Dutch American community (and their own part of it) that they have ceased to do much, if any, active propagation of the Christian faith. The Home Missions leaders see their problem: how to remain indigenous and at the same time become ardently evangelistic and effectively evangelistic....Naturally, we shall be talking with them about extension evangelism as well as expansion evangelism (February 26, 1974).[10]

Now, it should be pointed out that Dr. McGavran is well aware of the widespread outreach of the CRC through its radio outreach, *The Back to God Hour*. He is also grateful to God for its foreign mission society. But when he takes the measure of what its local congregations are not doing, he cannot but conclude that they have a faulty understanding of the ministry as scripturally defined.

The CRC's ministry of evangelism and church planting (Item 6 on our diagram) is so marginal to its essence as a New Testament church, that one could almost say that apart from the desire of its Kuyperians to be salt in the earth, CRC theology is "a theology of the elect for the elect." Dr. McGavran would have this church enlarge her perspectives and rearrange her priorities until the dimension of mission is large and central. In my chapter in the McGavran *Festschrift* I sought to summarize his position as follows:

> God wills the growth of His church. A chief and irreplaceable element in her ministry is the proclamation of the Gospel to all mankind and incorporation of those who believe into her communal life. Only through the deliberate multiplication of vast numbers of new congregations all over the world will the church be able to evangelize this generation. When she ceases to perform this mission, something fundamental is lost in her very essence as the people of God in the

---

[10]Donald McGavran, memo, dated February 26, 1974 to his colleagues at the Fuller School of World Mission.

midst of the nations. The church that does not grow is out of the will of God.[11]

Fortunately, the Home Missions staff of the CRC has taken to heart this exposure to the emphases of Dr. McGavran and the Church Growth movement. After much reflection nine separate theses were drafted, then examined in the light of Scripture and the Reformed faith. They are worthy of our careful study since they are germane to our concern for the Reformed churches with which we are associated. However, we will only indirectly allude to them here. The final section of this paper will be a summarization of the emphases which should be examined by us at this conference. They follow in the form of definitions.

Church Growth—God wills it, and makes it possible!

Inasmuch as God wills the salvation of men (I Tim 2:4; II Pet. 3:9; John 3:16) it follows that God wills that his church grow. Since God wants his lost children found, and since the church is ideally the company of those who have been found, the evangelical church that grows in membership is providing an irresistible demonstration of the will of God being accomplished in its midst. Indeed, church growth is a test of the faithfulness of the people of God to the ministry to which he has called them.

The Gospels confront us again and again with the love of Christ for men. It was this love that ultimately led him to pour out His life a ransom for many. The crucifixion and resurrection of our Lord are inherent to the record of the gospel of Jesus Christ. And yet, the events surrounding his cross and empty tomb do not climax the gospel narratives. The climax is his issuance of the mandate to disciple the nations. And this mandate is to be obeyed. Jesus Christ expects us to give ourselves to the task of gathering the lost. An illustration would be found in Matthew 9:36; 10:15. In this passage he called not only his disciples to pray the Lord of the harvest to send out laborers into his harvest (v. 38), He also counted on them to spend themselves in the task of preaching the gospel of the kingdom (10:5-23).

Some years ago, after a class in Missions here at Westminster Theological Seminary, a student came up with a question. He faced me, tears gathering in his eyes. "I am preaching to a dying church. What should

---

[11]Alan R. Tippett, *God, Man and Church Growth: A Festschrift in Honor of Donald Anderson McGavran* (Grand Rapids: William B. Eerdmans Publishing Company, 1973), p. 52.

I do?" It so happened that I knew the church and years before had occasionally worshiped there. It was in a heavily populated city across the street from a church-related college. I asked. "Is it God's will for that church to die? It is almost the only evangelical church in a community of over 100,000 people." He quickly agreed that God could hardly want the church to die. I continued. "Do you believe He can and will enable that church to grow?" He found this hard to accept. I pressed on. "Will you accept the fact that you are doubtless the key to whether that church grows or not?" He nodded. "Even if this means that what you are now doing probably needs to be reviewed—for it doesn't seem to be producing the results God desires—and there is every possibility that He wants you to do something different from what you are now doing." I then went on to describe a church only six miles away in a similar community, but which was experiencing great growth. "Why don't you go and study that other church? God is enabling it to grow. Do you not think He would be glorified if you were to make such a study and apply the lessons you learn, believing that it is His will that your church likewise grow? And His enablement will make it grow?" The tragedy is that nothing came of my suggestion. The church died.

Part of the tragedy of the Christian church is that this has all too frequently happened down through her long history. And it is quite unnecessary. In this connection Dr. McGavran has said, "Granting that God is sovereign and man can neither make the church grow nor convert anyone ... we must nevertheless ask, 'How can we be better stewards of the grace of God?' The more we study the growth of churches the more we find cases when lack of growth is clearly the result of preventable human factors. Slow growth is a disease that can and should be cured."

The CRC report supports this judgment:

> It is an understatement to say that the Lord wills the church to grow. Our Lord does not simply wait for it to happen, nor will he let his disciples quietly wait. He personally takes the business in hand. As risen Lord he issues his proclamation of life-giving dominion and enables his disciples immediately to act on it. Through them he sets his sights large on mankind, brings the receptive under his love, perfects them in obedience, and builds them into a baptized fellowship.

> If Scripture assures us that God wills and energizes the body for multiplication, we must likewise desire and expect "daily additions of those being saved." God's willing and enabling are a mandate for the

church to do, lovingly and deliberately, everything necessary to bring unbelievers into its fellowship....[12]

The Call to Conversion—You must issue it!

Despite fallen man's desperate condition, guilty and defiled—without hope and without God—it is the gracious purpose of God to call from the nations a people for himself. He issues this call through the church's proclamation of the gospel. Hence, apart from the obligation and privilege of the people of God to worship Him (Item 1), Christian have no higher responsibility than to be His vehicle for seeking out men and women, and gathering them to Christ through the call to repentance and to faith. Dr. McGavran uses the words "chief" and "irreplaceable" to describe this central task. Only thereby will the church grow.

It is utterly essential that this task of calling people to repentance toward God and faith toward our Lord Jesus Christ (Acts 20:21; 26:20) be regarded as the indispensable element in the church's ongoing commitment to Christ's Lordship.

Although men are dead in trespasses and sins, their rational and volitional faculties have not been destroyed. They are addressable. They can be informed of God's truth for they are able to perceive its implications. Dr. McGavran never ceases to urge upon all Christians the apostolic example of pressing home on all men the claims of Christ. He refuses to give ground on this point. All who follow Christ are to expect Him to transform them into faithful witnesses to His love and grace. Whereas not all will have the gift for evangelism, all will receive grace from Him to confess His name before men.

But more, the church in issuing this call through its members must expect men to respond. The Gospel is not merely to be proclaimed; God intends it to be believed. If there was one unvarying characteristic of apostolic preaching, it was that a verdict was expected. The apostles were forthright in their conviction that God commands men to repent (Acts 17:30). And they looked for results.

When men repented the expectation was that a radical break would take place with their former pattern of self-centeredness and disobedience. When men exercised faith in the Lord Jesus the expectation was that a

---

[12] *On the Growing Church* A paper prepared for the Christian Reformed Board of Home Missions. (Grand Rapids, Michigan: Christian Reformed Church, 1974). Mimeographed. No pagination. (Pagination supplied by editor.) p. 5.

Christ-centeredness would come to the center of their being. Indeed, the purpose of the gospel was to lead to faith, to rescue men from sin and death, and to make them new creatures in Christ.

Dr. McGavran would challenge the presumption of the church that regards itself as obedient to Christ if it fails to reach out after people with this gospel. He would deliberately overstate this by asking how it dares call itself the church. In his judgment and based on his long experience in India, the church committed to Christ will always find that its issuance of the call to repentance and faith, in season and out of season, is part of the essentiality of its ongoing life of total commitment. As the CRC report states:

> Early Christians saw mankind as lost, endangered by judgment. Their lively awareness of the unevangelized under peril outweighed any hesitation that the scandal of Christ's particularity may have caused them. They realized man's destiny hinged on response to their message. Their mission proceeded in the light of eternity, under the scrutiny of God as Savior and Judge.... Early church evangelism is a permanent reminder of the church's first priority.... When the clear call to conversion and obedience is minimized, the unique strategy of the Christian faith has been exchanged for something else. God ordained the church primarily for seeking the lost and bringing them into his Kingdom. [13]

Structuring for Evangelism—Beware of Introversion!

In 1955, Dr. McGavran published *Bridges of God,* a book that gave him worldwide prominence. One of its controversial issues was the distinction he made between the two forces that continually press themselves upon the church—discipling the nations (mission) and perfecting the inner life of the congregation (nurture). Although he contended that both have validity (according to our diagram of $\delta\iota\alpha\kappa o\nu\iota\alpha$: Items 1, 2 & 3 versus 6,) Dr. McGavran felt:

> There is a constitutional bias toward perfecting; the churches gravitate toward caring for what they have. Their inbuilt nature prefers perfection to mission. [14]

---

[13] *Ibid.,* pp. 6, 8.
[14] Donald A. McGavran, *Bridges of God; A Study in the Strategy of Missions"* (New York: Friendship Press, 1955), p.33

We readily assent. The average church utilizes the voluntary assistance of scores of its members to make possible its Sunday services and its weekday program. Dr. McGavran calls this "Class 1 activity." He defends its importance because he recognizes that without it the congregation could not function: the church school would not be staffed, the choir would be without members, and there would be neither deacons nor elders to conduct the temporal and spiritual affairs of the Lord's people.

Unfortunately, this type of activity inevitably gets out of hand. The church becomes introverted and preoccupied with itself. Selfishness takes over. Here is where Dr. McGavran moves in and challenges the congregation to take stock of the actual number of people and the amount of time spent in this "maintenance" activity, alongside the number of people and amount of time spent in evangelism. This leads him to ask a most basic question. How can a church grow if it is preoccupied with itself?

As a solution, Dr. McGavran would call for a careful review of the emphases of the pulpit ministry. Is the mandate for evangelism and mission being pressed home on the hearts and consciences of the people? Are one and all being taught the biblical principles and apostolic practice of seeking the lost and gathering them into congregations? If all are subjected to this training, eventually those peculiarly gifted by God for outreach will be discovered. Their combined energies can then be channeled into projects of near-neighbor evangelism, the planting of new congregations around home Bible study groups, and advanced training for yet more effective outreach. Dr. McGavran calls this Class II activity. He contends that unless it is structured into the life of the congregation only biological and transfer growth will take place, not conversion growth. The CRC report confirms the wisdom of this structured changes in the stance of the congregation.

> If growth is natural for an organism such as Christ's body, and if reaching the lost is the church's clear priority, then discipleship training also must find its source and direction in that mission. Where a church concentrates its training resources on introspection and a continual perfecting, it faces the danger of standing in splendid solitude. The result then may only be "Christian" ghettoism. Insistence that the congregation must first be built up internally, before vigorous evangelism training is undertaken, yields a church where evangelism is only a sideline. With millions still not found and gathered into the church, an over-riding sense of urgency must infect all discipleship education. And this fullness of heart, in turn, must be channeled into articulate and effective speech....In order to serve the

God who "desires all men to be saved" (I Tim. 2:4) concern for and skills in the salvation of others must saturate the curriculum and become instilled in every member.[15]

Training in Evangelism—Why Criticize Contemporary Methods?

Christians participate in Christ and with one another. By the Holy Spirit they share a common life. It is this which makes the service of Christ so exciting. Life lives and moves, and reaches out and multiplies. It cannot be contained. This is the dominant impression one gains of the church in the early chapters of the Acts. Those believers needed no instruction in evangelism. The flame went from heart to heart, from city to countryside, even to the despised Samaritans.

To speak in this fashion is to overlook the fact that the early disciples had been trained in our Lord's school of evangelism. He had given them both methods and models. They were not without considerable evangelistic "know-how" on the day the Spirit came to them. Later, He gave Paul the successive steps to take with those He would seek to evangelize (Acts 26:18).

It is tragic that those committed to the Reformed faith all too often summarily dismiss the canned approaches used by vigorous movements in our day. We rationalize: "Jesus employed a different approach with each person; He dealt with no two seekers alike." And yet, the fact remains that in our day the Holy Spirit has been pleased to bless persistently and abundantly the evangelistic movements that employ and advocate such methods. "Everyone is dumped into one mold; creativity is being stifled"— we growl on and on.

How would Dr. McGavran react to this? He might draw our attention to Luke 10:1-12 and ask us some pointed questions. What steps did Jesus take to send out the seventy? What definite instruction and specific guidelines did he provide? The hour was late, the need for many witnesses was urgent. Did he send them forth equipped with only the ABC's of evangelism, expecting that with the passage of time and their acquisition of experience each of the seventy would begin increasingly to make his own adaptations of his primary instruction?

Obviously, Dr. McGavran knows a great deal about the evangelistic movements of our day, their weaknesses as well as their strengths. And yet if he finds you standing on the sideline finding fault with their theology and

---

15 *On the Growing Church*, op. cit., p. 12.

their methods, but doing little to evangelize others he will press you to forget your prejudices and enroll in a program in order to get an inside perspective. Many Christians have been enabled to embark on a life of vigorous, mature, and effective confession of Christ by beginning with something canned. Try it, you'll like it. The CRC report summarizes:

> Thus, each Christian in his own way will inevitably respond, react, witness, evangelize—in all kinds of ways that uniquely show his life in Jesus Christ. By divine intention and provision Christianity is contagious material. Where evangelism activities are non-existent, or desultory rather than spontaneous, a prime necessity for that church is to begin "with deliberate haste" to structure itself for evangelism. If it hasn't happened unselfconsciously, then it must happen selfconsciously until the church has again trained itself in the habits of reaching out in Christ's name to the lost. Constant restructuring, adapting, and organizational shifting are always essential if the church is to move according to its nature, if life is to proceed freely and genuinely through it to the world.[16]

Priority in Evangelism—Concentrate on the Responsive!

Dr. McGavran contends that evangelistic and missionary policy should be based on two assumptions: (a) that the masses are growing increasingly responsive and will continue to listen to the Good News just because many influences bearing on their lives will make them increasingly dissatisfied with their present status, and (b) that particular peoples in certain countries and sections of countries fluctuate in response as they are played upon by military fortune, economic forces, victories and defeats.[17]

Although, at first reading this seems highly arbitrary, one cannot explore with Dr. McGavran this principle of "winning the winnable while they are winnable" without becoming aware of the profound theological issues that have led him to this formulation. Dr. McGavran's evangelical theology makes large room for the reality of God's sovereignty in election. He is no unthinking activist approaching the evangelistic task with the simplistic aim of loving the sinner, and seeking his conversion by whatever method works. Dr. McGavran teaches that man is utterly lost apart from God and cannot be saved apart from his grace. Further, he is fully aware that no man comes to the Lord Jesus unless the Father draws him (John 6:44).

---

[16] *Ibid,* pp. 10, 11.

[17] Donald A. McGavran, *Understanding Church Growth* (Grand Rapids, Michigan: William B. Eerdmans Publishing House, 1970), p. 256.

Hence, he rejects the pietism that says, "Go where you are sent even if you cannot expect a harvest." He reasons, If God is selective in His grace, if Jesus Christ in the days of His flesh deliberately bypassed some to reach others, should not His servants expect His Spirit to lead them to concentrate on the responsive (Matt. 9:13; Luke 9:5)? He asks, Did the apostle Paul uniformly go to the cities? Hardly! Actually, he concentrated on the Gentile "Godfearers" who ringed the Jewish synagogues of the Mediterranean world. As someone has facetiously said, "Paul was not so much a church-planter as a synagogue-splitter." Paul's God was not uniformitarian but selective (Rom. 9:14-18). He chose Jacob in preference to Esau. He constrained some to believe but Pharaoh's heart he hardened. And when Paul faced an unresponsive Jewish community in Pisidian Antioch he had but one final, terrible word for them, "It was necessary that the Word of God should be spoken first to you. Since you thrust it from you, and judge yourselves unworthy of eternal life, behold we turn to the Gentiles" (Acts 13:46).

When Dr. McGavran speaks of the selectivity of God and calls us to plan our evangelistic outreach with this in mind, he is being sensitive to the wonder of Sovereign grace. Little is to be gained by seeking to probe the mystery of God's inscrutable will. Dr. McGavran strongly resists those who rationalize their passivity in issuing the call to conversion by appealing to the doctrine of predestination. If it be the duty of all men to repent and believe the Gosepl, then it is the duty of those entrusted with the gospel to endeavor to make it known to all men. Since God alone makes men responsive, we should go where God has begun this prior work.

There is a time when God's Spirit is peculiarly active in the hearts of men. They become "ripe unto harvest." As a result, all evangelistic activity should be in response to an awareness of where God is at work. Down through the years, as a result of a great deal of "soil testing" and field research, we have found that wherever this empirical factor has been deliberately made determinative of strategy, God has abundantly confirmed with good harvests. Indeed we feel we have leaped over the inscrutable mystery that down through the years has provoked endless theological debate and ecclesiastical division, and have put our strength where it furthers, not hinders, the ongoing of the Christian mission. In seeking to win those whom God has made winnable we have not unnaturally gained new insight into what it means to be co-laborers with God in the building of his Church.

As Dr. McGavran would say, "Go to the masses! It should not be mission policy to besiege indifferent and resistant or even rebellious segments of the human mosaic because they are prestige-laden elements of their societies. God is able to raise up men of prestige from the very stones—the rejected, the disinherited, and the things which are not— provided they become members of his household."[18]

The CRC report supports this thesis:

> Not everyone responds in faith. Why do some accept the gospel and others reject it? In what proportion does this occur? Some kinds of soil do not produce. There are people who decline the banquet invitation. For many the cost of discipleship becomes too great when judged by their scale of values. The gospel presses men into a yes or no, so we cannot be indifferent to the patterns of decision....

> There is no universal strategy, no single gimmick that works everywhere. If we monitor our own effectiveness, we can be prepared to change our tactics and approach (though not our message) whenever necessary....

> We should not be afraid to pioneer or on the other hand to admit that some particular effort has not produced the hoped-for results. Where correction is needed or change of direction is required, let it be done. Sometimes a new day and a new hour will demand radical change for constructive labor. Our Lord does not expect us to remain forever where He is not wanted (Matt. 10:14).

> Whereas God's Word is appropriate to every person in all ages and circumstances, making accurate assessments of the area and situation will prevent wasted effort and facilitate the Word's movement. There is an abundance of opportunity confronting the church today. As we reach out to that world we must learn to know it as it is in reality. Our understanding of that world plays a large role in our dedication to and fulfillment of mission.[19]

Unity with Diversity—Are Cultural Distinctives Wrong?

Dr. McGavran is forever mounting campaigns against the use of inexact terms, vague generalizations, and what he calls "foggy language." Not *fruit* but something specific like apples, peaches and pears. Not *people,* but Hindu-speaking, middle-class Hindus or Kakka-speaking village Chinese.

---

[18] *Ibid.,* p. 257.
[19] *On the Growing Church,* op. cit., 17, 18.

Not *urbanites* but the separate peoples that make up the mosaic of people living in a particular city. Not *church* but the basic building block or homogeneous unit (HU) characterizing a particular congregation.

Dr. McGavran is continuously on the lookout for the separate characteristics of each section of society, whether ethnic, linguistic, political, geographic, economic, social. Why so? Because the church never grows among mankind in general; it always grows in a homogeneous unity, and according to the specific pattern of that homogeneous unit.

Nothing is more important than identifying the homogeneous unit (or units) that make up a specific congregation. Once identified its distinctive characteristics must be carefully researched until its inner ethos and elan are fully appreciated. If a congregation is conglomerate, the probability is that it is growing slowly. The more each homogeneous unit congregation is encouraged to maintain its own distinctives, the more attractive it will be to members of that homogeneous unit yet to be converted. An important principle of church growth is that "discipling each homogeneous unit out to the fringes is more desirable as a rule than establishing conglomerate congregations in many contiguous HUs."

Dr. McGavran sees the picture: "When each unit has a cluster of vigorous congregations in its midst made up exclusively of its own folk, then becoming Christian involves neither denying one's own HU, nor traitorously joining a strange people. The decision to become a disciple of Christ is then solely a religious decision. In contrast, however, if homogeneous units are disregarded and churches established in many of these so that becoming a Christian gets the image of 'leaving your unit for a larger conglomerate mongrel whole,' then two things happen, (a) the resulting church is weak, is split by factions and is an organization rather than an organism; (b) the resulting conglomerate churches find it difficult to grow because every invitation to 'love the Lord and follow Him' sound like an invitation to 'leave your brethren and join ours'."[20]

As was to be expected, this concept has been hotly challenged on theological grounds by those who contend that it perpetuates the fragmentation of the human race. Has not Christ removed the barriers between men, making unity out of diversity? In reply, Dr. McGavran would inquire as to the precise meaning that Scripture would have us attach to this oneness. Does the gospel obliterate all distinctives, or does

---

[20]Donald A. McGavran, "The Homogeneous Unit in Mission Theory," (a paper delivered at the annual meeting of the American Society of Missiology, St. Louis, Missouri, 1972), p. 52.

God allow for cultural and ethnic diversity in His church? Is God pleased with the solidly Dutch ethnicity of many CRC churches? Does he want these Dutch cultural patterns imposed on CRC congregations made up of Italians? Must there be an imperialistic uniformity in which the distinctions of males and females, Jews and Gentiles, slaves and free men are all removed (Gal. 3:28)? Or is it the Lord's intent that the unity overarching the diversity be a unity in the Spirit?

Dr. McGavran would summarize: "As I read the future many homogeneous units are fighting a losing battle against the tide in human affairs. They will eventually go. Larger and larger racial and linguistic unities appear likely. But homogeneous units are here now and are likely to be here for a long time. Let the church disciple each of them out to the fringes, operate with them, and preserve te richness of their cultures, and as far as it can mitigate the antipathy which rises between bodies of men, and promote love and justice between all men. The church working thus with the homogeneous unit not against it, will liberate the multitudinous ethnic units of mankind into the glorious liberty of the children of God."[21]

The CRC report confirms this thesis:

> The world is filled with an endless variety of people, all with a multiplied richness and varied hues and differing backgrounds. As we consider this multifaceted scene, we affirm our conviction that all those who profess the name of Jesus Christ are one, and members of one church (John 10:16; 17:21).

> But conversion to the Christian faith does not mean that a person must abandon his cultural distinctiveness and become culturally neutral or multicultural, even if such things were possible (Acts 15:28, 29).

> Those who receive the gospel tend to gravitate toward their own kind, within family patterns and familiar communities. Ever since Paul found himself in a vigorous movement of natural human connections, people movements on every continent and in all periods of history so testify and do it unmistakeably. The fact is that when homogeneous units are ignored, church growth is slowed and we have not utilized an important dimension of man's makeup.

> The goal, therefore, should be to establish churches which reflect and serve their community, each adapted and peculiar. Everyone then has something precious to offer, and the faith of the Christian community

---

[21] *Ibid.,* p. 56.

as a whole is enriched proportionately as increasing numbers of cultures are penetrated by the gospel and take their places within the orbit of the Christian religion. Out of many cultures the one universal church, a rich mixture of peoples, rises from its many cells and congregations and meeting places to serve her risen Lord.[22]

Conclusion

Obviously, in this paper we have only touched on some of the primary emphases of the theological and methodological perspectives of Dr. McGavran. We could have detailed his long struggle to convince missionaries of the wisdom of abandoning the "mission station" pattern of the 19th century. We could have reviewed his world-wide journeys with their pattern of research-cum workshop to establish the validity of the "people movement" and stimulate missionaries with the exciting possibilities of this method for discipling large numbers of people. We could have sought to catch the full measure of his courageous confrontations of the conciliar movement and its recent attempts to reconceptualize the missionary task into something quite foreign to the plain instruction of Scripture.

However, it has seemed more important that we concentrate on matters directly applicable to our Reformed movement in America. For it appears to me that we should be concerned that in these days of unparalleled receptivity, our churches gather in more of the harvest that stands ripened throughout our land.

---

[22] *On the Growing Church,* op. cit., pp. 14-16.

CHAPTER THREE

WINNABLE PEOPLE

by Roger S. Greenway*

From the outside the building looks more like a gymnasium, or even a giant warehouse, than an evangelical church. But when it is dedicated on March 31, 1976, its seating capacity of 25,000 will make it the largest church building in the world.

The Brazilian Pentecostal Church known as *Brazil for Christ,* founded by Manoel de Mello, two decades ago, has about 250,000 baptized members and is now in the process of spreading from its center in the city of Sao Paulo into the interior of Brazil. The new building will more than triple the number of people who can attend De Mello's services at the "mother church" and will greatly expand the training facilities for the hundreds of workers whom De Mello sends out to plant satellite churches in urban and rural areas.

Recently, a group of us visited the *Brazil for Christ* center in Sao Paulo and a friendly and enthusiastic member of the movement showed us around the buildings. He said that one hundred and five adult converts had been baptized the previous month and one hundred students were enrolled in the nine-month leadership training course. If we arrived with any doubts as to the Church's interest in culture and education we were in for some surprise, for our guide took us through two floors of the front part of the old building which are rented to the University of Sao Paulo five evenings a week for night classes which the Church members are urged to attend.

Roger Greenway has served as Latin America Secretary for the Board of Foreign Missions of the Christian Reformed Church since 1972. His missionary career began in 1958 when, appointed by his church, he served as collegiate minister of the Dutch Reformed Church in Sri Lanka (then Ceylon). In 1963, he was transferred to Mexico City to teach at the Juan Calvino Seminary. He received his doctorate in Missions from the Southwestern Baptist Theological Seminary, Forth Worth, Texas.

For several minutes I stood alone in the place where the pulpit would be located in the new auditorium. I looked over that vast area, not yet entirely roofed over, and I was awed by the thought that tens of thousands would hear the Gospel from that place. As I stood there I prayed that the messages that would be preached would ever be God's Word and that the crowds that would come would be taught the whole counsel of God.

Then another thought came to me. It was a disturbing one: If large numbers of people are ready to receive the Gospel today, why aren't Reformed mission endeavors meeting with this kind of response? Why isn't there somewhere in Latin American a Reformed Church erecting a church auditorium seating 25,000 people? Is Reformed theology inimical to church growth of this proportion? Or are we doing some wrong things, things which dishonor God as well as hinder church growth? Are there lessons, perhaps, which we can learn from movements like Brazil for Christ?

These are questions which needle Reformed missionaries, mission executives, professors of missions, and all who are burdened for the evangelization of the world but see relatively slow growth in their own mission endeavors. New and dynamic religious movements in certain parts of the world generally make Reformed church growth look pale and anemic. We conscientiously ask, *Why?*

The Church Growth Movement

For two decades there has been a self-conscious school of thought called the Church Growth movement. No other group of people in modern times has done more to stimulate thinking and writing on the subject of mission theory and methodology as have Dr. Donald A. McGavran and those associated with him in the Church Growth school. Compared to the amount of material produced by Reformed missiologists, Church Growth writers have been amazingly prolific. It is not surprising, therefore, that their ideas have found their way into almost every corner of the missionary world.

The Church Growth school of missiology makes a profession of asking probing questions concerning missionary methods and results. It calls for well-defined evangelistic goals and asks that the results of all missionary activity be measured over against these goals. In the words of Peter Wagner, "the Church Growth school ruthlessly evaluates strategies against objectives."[1]

[1]Peter Wagner, "Sharpening Issues in Church Growth," Pasadena, 1974, p. 13. (Mimeographed.)

Where steady, healthy growth is discovered Church Growth researchers seek out the factors contributing to this development and share the news with all who are eager to learn. But where methods are shown to be ineffective, Church Growth people urge that changes be made.

This naturally constitutes a threat to field missionaries and board executives that have been deeply committed to a certain program, particularly if the program has been used to raise funds and recruit new workers in the homeland. As Wagner says:

> Some programs have been hallowed with age and are being maintained at all costs, even though their effectiveness for evangelism has long since diminished. When church growth research uncovers such programs and attempts to make an objective analysis as to the reasons for their impotence, feelings of workers involved in them are often rubbed raw, and those of us associated with the church growth movement have consequently become the object of severe attacks.

> However, whereas some conclusions in church growth research are necessarily negative, as far as I know the *motivation* for such research has always been positive. Criticisms, when made, are meant to be constructive, although at times more diplomacy and tact could undoubtedly be employed in communicating them to persons involved. Where feelings are hurt because of blundering communicators, apologies are in order. It must be admitted that this is too often the case. But where feelings are merely symptoms of stubborn resistance to the kind of change that will help winnable men and women find Christ as their Savior, church growth advocates will typically promote that change despite hurt feelings which may result. In such cases criticism is considered a low price for the eternal salvation of the lost.[2]

The purpose of this inquiry is to discover where and how Church Growth principles and methods may help Reformed mission leaders carry out their task more responsibly to the glory of God. The Church Growth school of missiology did not spring from Reformed theology, though men of Reformed convictions are actively involved in it. A perusal of Church Growth literature from Donald A. McGavran's *The Bridges of God* in 1955 to Alan R. Tippett's *God, Man, and Church Growth,* a *Festschrift* published in McGavran's honor in 1973, reveals that Church Growth writers take seriously the importance of having a sound biblical theology underlying mission principles and practices. At the same time it is obvious

---

[2] *Ibid.*

that most of Church Growth missiology's theological bases have been worked out *after* the methodological insights and mission principles were arrived at through field observation and experience. Very often they were defined more in opposition to the arguments raised by the opponents of Church Growth than in relation to a recognized system of theology.

This, however, should not deter us from appropriating many of the valuable insights which the Church Growth school has laid hold upon and incorporating them into a Reformed system of thought. There are a number of biblical and practical insights in Church Growth writing which fairly cry for attention on the part of Reformed missiologists. Dr. Harry R. Boer has pointed out that "The great merit of McGavran in emphasizing the place of the *oikos* in missionary strategy can hardly be overestimated."[3] The Reformed doctrine of the covenant surfaces immediately when we examine Dr. McGavran's emphasis upon the family, the household, and the way in which the Holy Spirit works among people who are organically related to one another. When Church Growth theorists say that historically the Christian faith has spread via "chains of families," it comes as no surprise to Reformed people who have believed all along that God works covenantally through believers and their families. The sovereignty of God in election and providence is another distinctively Reformed emphasis which speaks to many of the issues raised by the Church Growth school, and particularly to the subject which is before us now. If there are more winnable people than ever before, it is the sovereign God who has made them so and it is the church's duty to recognize what He is doing and respond obediently.

As we attempt, therefore, to analyze certain aspects of Church Growth missiology from a Reformed perspective for the benefit of Reformed missions, our attitude is positive. Positive and also humble, for we must confess that in too many cases Reformed missionary achievements are small when compared to what certain groups have done whose theology and organization we regard as seriously deficient but whose accomplishments as far as the spread of the Gospel is concerned far exceed our own. We come to our subject prepared to learn, to analyze, to evaluate, and perhaps to repent if in the course of these studies we discover things we have done, or left undone, which have hindered the Gospel's free course in the world.

---

[3]Harry R. Boer: *Pentecost and Missions* (Grand Rapids: William B. Eerdmans Publishing Co., 1961), p. 184.

Are There More Winnable People Than Ever Before?

We will now address ourselves to this question in particular. The enthusiastic optimism of the Church Growth school is plainly articulated by Dr. Donald McGavran when he says:

> More winnable people live in the world today than ever before. India has far more now than in the days of Carey or Clough. Africa has myriads who can be won. Latin America teems with opportunity. For the Gospel, never before has such a day of opportunity dawned.[4]

The attitude of optimism which is so characteristic of Church Growth thinking, strikes a responsive chord among Reformed thinkers. For it is one of the first principles of missions that God is sovereign over the universe and in God's own time rebellious creation will be brought to its knees before him. Satan and his kingdom, strong as they are, are not equal contestants over against the Lord in the spiritual warfare that is missions. The forces of darkness are infinitely outmatched by God's grace and power. Missions, therefore as God's undertaking must succeed, and optimism is completely in order for all who stand on the Lord's side. With the Church Growth school we affirm that God is working out His strategy and nothing Satan can do will prevent Him from winning the victory.

It is important, I believe, to assert this theocentric viewpoint at the beginning of a missiological discussion. Missions is from God, through God, and unto God. Common as it is to begin from an anthropocentric, soteriocentric, or an ecclesiocentric, viewpoint, the Reformed missiologist defends the primacy of the sovereign God and His will and operation. If new things are happening today, it is ultimately God who is doing them and they are evidences of His on-going campaign against Satan's kingdom. If the ranks of Christ's army of righteousness are growing stronger it is because God is vindicating His honor through the salvation of sinners and the growth of His Church.

In pursuit of our answer to the question as to whether there are more winnable people than ever before we must come to grips with the meaning given to the qualifying adjective, *winnable*. A misunderstanding as to the meaning of "winnableness" could have serious consequences. I want to point out first of all, therefore, what we do *not* mean when we affirm that there are more winnable people in the world than ever before. After

---

[4]Donald A. McGavran, *Understanding Church Growth* (Grand Rapids: William B. Eerdmans Publishing Co., 1970), pp. 58-59.

examing the negative side we will proceed to consider the positive side of the question.

First of all, when we say that there are more winnable people in the world today we do not mean that men and women are less depraved, less involved in sin and idolatry, and therefore more inclined to love God and obey His word. The depravity of sin is just as real as it ever was and, in fact, there is evidence which suggests that rather than improving in his moral and spiritual condition man is entering an even more advanced stage in his rebellion against God and rejection of God's law. This spiritual and moral decline has many effects. The curse which God pronounced when sin first entered the world (Gen. 3:17; 5:29) is still active. As sin increases, the quality of human life and civilization decline and all that man has striven to achieve throughout history slips from his grasp. If men today are more winnable it is not because they are better. The opposite is more likely true.

Neither do we mean that the kingdom of darkness is beginning to show some gray areas, some lighter shadows which might lead us to greater optimism respecting man's winnableness. Satan remains the prince of this world and he is as preoccupied as ever by the thought of supplanting God in every part of the universe and of maintaining his control over man. Satan's hold is not slipping, nor are his intentions less malignant. His great objective was and still is to supplant God as the Ruler of the universe, and he uses men as the means to that end.

We must bear in mind that these "winnable" people about whom we are inquiring are Satan's weapons against God. Satan seduces and subjects man in order to attack God and defend himself from God. In the beginning, God made man the organic and legal head of creation. Man was the crown of creation, God's special handiwork and made in His image. Man also received a mandate reserved for him alone, that of being God's vice-agent in charge of all that God has made. This position of dominion made man of special interest to Satan who, having been expelled from heaven, aspired to dominion on earth. Satan brought man under his control, and subsequently has worked all kinds of havoc in the earth, not because he was primarily interested in being man's ruler but because he desired to use man to assert his own authority over what was rightfully God's domain. Having failed in heaven, he turned his attention to earth. Satan recognized that Adam held the key to God's creation-garden, and that by seducing Adam he could gain entrance. He succeeded in this, and having entered God's creation he refuses to depart. Satan became the prince of this world by usurpation. His ultimate downfall is sure (John 12:31), but he never gives up one soul or one inch of territory without a struggle. In opposition to Satan and his kingdom the light of the Gospel must shine forth as brilliantly as ever. Its message must be proclaimed in utter contrast to Satan's lie. If men in greater number are approachable and winnable today, it is not because Satan is losing interest in holding them captive or his kingdom showing some brighter spots. On that score there have been no changes.

Still another distinction must be made. When we say that there are more winnable people than ever before we must not leave the impression that in our estimation God's comprehensive plan for the universe is like a loose-leaf notebook to which in certain periods God may add some pages and include certain names which He did not have in mind before. On the contrary, God's plan is magnificent and totally comprehensive. He knew all the names, the places, and the events before it all began, and He accomplishes "all things according to the counsel of His will" (Ephesians 1:11).

God conceived the plan of missions before the world was made and to Him it is one organic whole. Though you and I see the plan executed piecemeal, so to speak, with unexpected changes from one age to the other, He sees the end from the beginning and knows how each event fits into the whole. If in His electing love more people today are to be won to faith and obedience, He planned it that way before the world began. It is no surprise to God.

Turning now to the positive side of the question, when we say with the Church Growth writers that there are more winnable people than ever before we mean first of all that more people are *accessible* than ever before. Earth's "remotest regions" are not as remote as they used to be. Travel is fast and relatively easy. Christian literature finds its way into lush high-rise apartments and seamy ghetto caverns. Technology has given the Church fantastic instruments for mass communication which can carry the Gospel to people who formerly were inaccessible. Today, people in isolated mountain villages are listening to God's Word as it is broadcast to them by radio or brought by way of cassette recordings. All of this was impossible during the first nineteen centuries of Christian missions. As far as the potential for reaching multitudes for Christ, our's is the greatest era in history.

I want to give a few illustrations at this point drawn from recent experiences of the Board of Foreign Missions of the Christian Reformed Church. We have a small but wonderfully successful mission enterprise operating in the Central American country of Honduras. Our work began in Honduras through contacts made by our denominational radio broadcast, *The Back to God Hour,* in Spanish. The weekly sermons of the Rev. Juan Boonstra were heard and appreciated by a group of people in Honduras' capital, Tegucigalpa. They began holding Sunday services and adopted the name "The Christian Reformed Church of Tegucigalpa." After taking this step they wrote to the Chicago office of *The Back to God Hour* and invited someone from our Church to visit them. We now have two missionaries working with this group and besides the "mother" church in the downtown area there are four other congregations meeting in the suburbs.

The same thing is happening on the island of Trinidad. There too a group of people has been listening to *The Back to God Hour* and have formed what they call "The Christian Reformed Church of Trindad." We are supplying them with printed materials for the purpose of instructing them in Reformed doctrine and church order. Personal visits may begin later this year.

In our generation, God seems to have given to the Pentecostals the special gift of winning many to the initial stages of Christian discipleship. But the Pentecostals as a rule lack the gift of teaching. Their preaching usually is superficial and their theological understanding meager. It is at this point that Reformed missions may be able to exercise a very important ministry if we recognize the opportunities and respond to them relevantly. The following excerpt is taken from a letter sent to me by the Rev. Arnold Rumph, one of our missionaries in Puerto Rico. The Rev. Rumph handles correspondence from the Caribbean for *The Back to God Hour.* Before this letter was written he had received an invitation from a group of believers in the Dominican Republic who had no relationship with any denomination and wanted to organize themselves as a Christian Reformed Church. These people were of a somewhat Pentecostal background but they were impressed by the preaching they heard on *The Back to God Hour* broadcast and had decided to identify themselves with the denomination that sponsored it.

We had a service on Sunday morning from 9:30 until 12:15. It was quite a moving experience for me. A total of 21 people were present, 2 of them children, 6 women and 13 men. One of the men, the secretary, taught the Sunday school lesson in a very simple way but he did it very effectively asking many questions and getting a lot of feed-back from the people. And he really taught the Bible. I preached and at their request explained to them the basic doctrines of the Iglesia Cristiana

Reformada. We certainly had a wonderful time of fellowship. I was particularly impressed by the fact that there were so many men in church in comparison to the women and children. The secretary handed me a list of the membership of the church. It appears that about 55 people are members or sympathizers. They told me that many that day could not come because they had to work (most of the people work in the sugar cane industry). Well, it may be a church that has a very elementary understanding of the Reformed faith but as far as I know it's the first Iglesia Cristiana Reformada in the Dominican Republic. I promised them that I would try to supply them with biblical material (Heidelberg Catechism, books like *De Todo Corazon,* some Bibles in Spanish and some New Testaments in Creole, etc.) and keep regular contact with them by means of correspondence. I also said that I would propose to the Mission to visit them once or twice a year. They seemed to be very happy with these proposed arrangements. After the service I had coffee with them in the home of the pastor, a large wooden shack, and took some slides. I went back by "publico" to Santo Domingo, a hair-raising experience since the small Japanese car had packed in so many passengers that at times I hardly could breathe and we went with such a speed over the pot-holed roads that it's a miracle the car didn't disintegrate.

If ever we want to expand our missionary outreach I think that there are many opportunities in the Dominican Republic. The people there seem to be a lot more open to the Gospel then here in Puerto Rico. Moreover, as far as I know, there is no Reformed witness in the Dominican Republic. With a flexible set-up and the availability of educational help and periodic visits, I think that quite a few churches could be organized in the Dominican Republic.

I am fully aware of the problems which exist in trying to follow up contacts derived from mass communications such as radio, and the great importance of instructing new converts and developing congregations in the basic doctrines and practices of the faith through the personal ministry of one of God's servants present in their midst. But as a mission administrator and strategist I know that the opportunities are greater than our human resources can even begin to handle. We must fall back each day afresh to that utter dependency upon the Lord which the Apostle Paul expressed when he testified that all that he had said and done was in actual fact Christ's accomplishment through him in leading the Gentiles to obey God (Romans 15:18).

The second thing we mean when we say that there are more winnable people than ever before is that never since the days of the Roman Empire have there been so many people craving for the peace and justice which only Christ and His Kingdom can supply. I have alluded to this earlier and now I want to explain what I mean more fully. That we live in an age of revolution is obvious to all of us. Against what are men revolting? When we look at Latin America, for example, what are the masses searching for, reacting against, and hoping to achieve? Is it not justice that they seek, and freedom from oppression the thing they crave? Foul systems, both foreign and domestic, have ground their heels into the neck of the poor for so long that oppression seems almost ineradicable and injustice the normal way of life. Today, millions of people are deciding that they have had enough. They are willing to shed blood, their own as well as that of others, to tear down the systems that enslave them in the hope that something better will take their place. The banners they follow are vague and uncertain and may lead them to greater misery than they knew before. But they follow them anyway, in search of a "savior" and a just society which will fulfill their needs.

I see this as a sign that God, with a redemptive purpose, is stirring the nations to seek the righteous kingdom of which Christ is the Head. The two conflicting poles of contemporary politics, communism on the left and fascism on the right, and all that lies between them, cannot satisfy the souls and minds of men. Wretched ones caught in the turmoil of revolution do not know where the answer lies. But we do. It lies with Christ and His Kingdom. As Reformed missiologists we should view the contemporary world as a world filled with unique missionary opportunities, particularly for us who insist that Christ's sovereignty must be recognized in all spheres of life. Now is the time to make the Reformed viewpoint heard.

Besides the craving for change and a social order that is more just and satisfying, there is the factor of cultural disintegration in many parts of the world.

In the first volume of his seven-volume study entitled *A History of the Expansion of Christianity,* Kenneth Scott Latourette describes the environment into which Christianity was born in God's "fullness of time." The Mediterranean basin formed the center of the most powerful and complex culture man had yet developed. But one of the significant factors in the situation was that cultural disintegration was occurring during the time when Christianity experienced its most rapid spread. Latourette points out that cultural change and disintegration in the ancient world provided an opportunity for the growth of the new faith among vast numbers of people. He explains this by saying:

Never has Christianity been adopted where the pre-Christian culture remained intact. In some regions of high civilizations, as in Persia, India, China, and Japan, it has won the allegiance of minorities. It has often obtained the adherence of entire peoples of primitive or nearly primitive cultures, but only as these peoples, in accepting it, abandoned their own culture and adopted, at least in part, that with which Christianity was associated.

Even in the Graeco-Roman world cultural disintegration had set in before Christianity attracted more than a minority. It was largely because the established civilization was dissolving, weakened by many other factors than the attack of Christianity, that the faith was able to win.[5]

Many parallels can be drawn between the situation which existed during the first three centuries of the Christian era and the contemporary world scene. There is the worldwide dissemination of Western civilization with its parallels in Greek culture, as well as cultural disintegration and widespread hunger for something new and more satisfying. Traditional societies everywhere are undergoing traumatic changes, and patterns of life and religion which for centuries prevented people from hearing or taking seriously the message of Christianity are breaking down. People in a hundred lands are open to new ideas, including religious ideas. They dare to acquire Bibles, attend church services, and openly profess Christian discipleship without fear of reprisals from the community. All this is due to the fact that established cultures are disintegrating and old ties are being broken.

Nowhere is this occuring faster than in the great urban centers. Ours will soon be an *urban* world. At the beginning of the twentieth century, only about thirteen percent of the world's population lived in towns and cities. All the rest lived in rural areas and their labor was closely related to agriculture and the soil. By the end of the twentieth century the situation will be completely reversed and only thirteen percent of the world's population will be classed as living in rural areas, and eighty-seven percent will live in urban and metropolitan centers. Living as we do in the midst of this change it is hard to comprehend what it all means and what long-range effects it will have on the universal spread of Christianity. But we have a

[5]Kenneth Scott Latourette, The First Five Centuries, Vol. 1 of *A History of the Expansion of Christianity* (New York: Harper and Brothers Publishers, 1937), p.7.

model to examine and it brings to light some fascinating insights. Mentally, let us translate Latourette's description of the cosmopolitan world which Christianity first entered into terms which fit our own day and situation:

> An outstanding characteristic of the world which entered was a growing cosmopolitanism. For at least three centuries before the birth of Christ this movement had been in progress. The Persian conquests had paved the way for it, but its inception is usually dated from Alexander the Great. Although the empire which he built broke apart almost immediately after his death, the spread of Hellenistic culture continued under the Greek rulers who made themselves heirs of the various portions of his realm. The Roman Empire occupied a much larger proportion of the Mediterranean basin than had Alexander. The unity of its government, the commerce and travel which it fostered, and its comparative tolerance furthered the disintegration of old cultural units. Greece and Rome were both city states. Alexander and his successors and the Romans, therefore, encouraged the founding and growth of cities. In a certain sense the Empire into which Christianity entered was a congeries of semi-autonomous cities held together by the rule of Rome. No longer, however, were they fully independent politically. Bound together by a growing commerce and under one central administration, in art, institutions, and ideas they tended to conform to one pattern. Local peculiarities were weakened. In this unified world, moreover, thousands of individuals were torn loose from their hereditary *milieu*. As merchants, as slaves, or as soldiers, they found themselves in alien environments. Uprooted from their accustomed soil, the migrants tended to borrow from one another and to abandon or alter their inherited cultures. The Roman Empire was a vast melting-pot in which each ingredient tended to modify and to be modified by every other. The city meant less to the citizen than it had in early Greek or Roman times. The individual often felt lost and sought solace in a religion adapted to his needs and in voluntary, unofficial organizations.[6]

It was not an accident that Christianity had most of its earliest strongholds in cities and from there spread out to conquer the countryside. Cities were the centers of change and communication. Commercial and cultural ties linked the cities of the ancient world together, and provided the natural channels for the faith to spread. In the cosmopolitan environment Christianity found masses of people caught in the bewildering labyrinth of city life and receptive to a new faith which met their spiritual needs and

---

[6] *Ibid.,* pp. 10, 11

offered them hope. The same conditions exist throughout much of the world today, and should pray — and expect — that the results will be even greater for the spread of Christianity.

This leads to my final observation which has to do with the *receptivity* to the Gospel which we find in a number of places today. We have said before that as time-bound people we see God's will for the ages unfolded piecemeal. It is all one unified plan to Him, but not to us. Just as His plan for one generation is not the same as for another, the number of His elect is not a static percentage figure for all times and places. Church Growth writers have served us well by reminding us that while certain lights may be dimming and even going out in one part of the world, new lights are appearing and burning brightly in others. If we take the broad view we cannot escape the conclusion that we live in the best century of all for the spread of the Gospel; and an even better one may lie ahead.

In conclusion I point to Africa, where in the words of David Barrett history's most massive influx into the churches is taking place.[7] The receptivity of modern Africans to the Gospel is revealed by the fact that there were only ten million Christians in Africa at the beginning of this century, but there were 130 million Africans that called themselves Christians in the census year of 1970. We cannot enter now into a discussion of the various reasons behind the fact that thirty million Africans who consider themselves Christians are not recognized as such by the established churches. That requires separate attention, and David Barrett has done his work well by providing us with enough data to justify the conclusion that while on the one hand this 30-million "fringe" group in Africa represents clear evidence of successful and ongoing Christian mission, it also represents a great tragedy in that thirty million willing and responsive people are kept dangling on the threshold of the church.

What is happening in Africa is taking place on various scales in other parts of the world in particular areas. Winnable, accessible, and responsive people are not found everywhere, but they are to be found in many places; more perhaps than we recognize. The Presbyterian churches of Korea have grown strong and numerous in this century and Korea seems to be well on the way to becoming a Christian nation. In spite of the fact that Burma is closed to missionaries, many tribal people are responding to the Gospel and churches are multiplying. Indonesia has been the scene of some

---

[7]David Barrett, "History's Most Massive Influx in the Churches," in *God, Man and Church Growth,* ed. by Alan R. Tippett (Grand Rapids: William B. Eerdmans Publishing Co., 1973), pp. 396-413.

remarkable revivals during the last decade and it is the one country in the world where Muslims in significant numbers have been won to Christ.

In Latin America some great things are happening and a brief look at the statistics will bring this out. At the beginning of this century there were only fifty thousand Protestants in Latin America. By 1930 there were one million, by 1940 two million, by the mid-1950s there were five million and in the 1960s ten million. Today there are more than twenty million Protestants in Latin America and some predict that there will be 100 million by the end of the century.

Are there more winnable people in the world today than ever before? There is much evidence to indicate that there are. We believe, moreover, that it is God who has made them winnable. The harvest is His and He has made it ripe. It is now our task, as the Lord's appointed reapers, to set forth a sound and well-defined theology upon which to base the work of evangelization, develop mission strategies in line with biblical principles and the realities of each field situation, deploy our resources to meet the challenges of ripened fields, raise up great armies of prayer-warriors throughout the churches, and pass on to the churches of Asia, Africa, and Latin America such a compassion for lost people and zeal for Christ's Gospel that they will enter with eagerness the great harvest which God has made ripe.

CHAPTER FOUR

THE PLACE AND IMPORTANCE OF NUMERICAL
CHURCH GROWTH

by John M. L. Young*

What is the paramount task of the church? Is the numerical growth of the church the supreme task of the church?

To the founder of the Church Growth movement, Donald McGavran, the answer to this question is clear: "Today's supreme task is effective multiplication of churches in the receptive societies of earth."[1] Again: "Today's paramount task, opportunity, and imperative in missions is to multiply churches in the increasing numbers of receptive peoples of the earth."[2]

The objective of this paper is to give serious consideration to the place and importance of numerical church growth. Let us begin then, by considering the place numerical growth should have in Christ's mission. For those who believe the scriptures to be the word of God, the answer will be sought there, and the effort will be made to frame a theological statement of the mission of the church reflective of their understanding of the Lord's instructions on the matter. Such a statement will inevitably also reflect the underlying theological position of the framer, his view of the nature of God and of man, the way they both operate, and their relation to

*John M. L. Young serves on the faculty of Covenant College, Tennessee, as Professor of Missions, a post he has filled since 1967. Born in Korea of Presbyterian missionary parents, he labored in Manchuria from 1938-1941, in China from 1948-1949, and in Japan from 1949-1966. During that time he participated in the founding of the Japan Christian Theological Seminary and served as its president from 1952-1966.

---

[1]Donald A. McGavran, *Understanding Church Growth* (Grand Rapids: Wm. B. Eerdmans Publishing Co., 1970) p. 49.

[2] *Ibid.*, p. 63.

each other. Important indeed to the laying of a foundation for a theology of missions are these matters and influential to the formation of a methodology of missions will be the theological answers given.

How, then does McGavran state his understanding of what the scriptures call for by way of the church's mission?"We may define mission narrowly," he states, "as *an enterprise devoted to proclaiming the good news of Jesus Christ and to persuading men to become his disciples and dependable members of his church.*" [3]

The word "persuade" is a key word in this definition. It becomes clear that what it means is not merely trying to convince one to do or believe, merely urging, but actually harvesting men into the church. This meaning is apparent in the differentiation made between "a theology of seed sowing" — "search theology," from a "theology of harvest" in which men are "found," that is "harvested." He writes: "In finding, God wants them *found* — that is brought into a redemptive relationship with Jesus Christ . . . ."[4]

The search theology is held to be inadequate for it is neutral towards results, "a neutralist position," and it takes the position that the church's "duty is complete in proclamation."[5] Those who consistently apply this search theology are then identified with the view: "God is taking out of the Gentiles a limited number of people to be his church. Nothing the missionary does can add to or subtract from his purpose."[6] Most sobering is the conclusion that although he sympathizes "with the purposes that inspire search theology, and with the limited truths it so often expresses," nonetheless, "we do not believe the neutralist position is theologically sound. It is out of harmony with the mainstream of Christian revelation. Christ's words and deeds contradict it. The apostles in the early church would have repudiated it."[7] The rejection of "the neutralist position" thus involves a rejection of the idea that the number God intends to save is fixed and cannot be added to or subtracted from.

The task set for the mission is the *effective* multiplication of churches in the receptive societies of the earth. These societies are also called responsive ones, "winnable" people over against "resistant" people. It is they who are to be found and made members of people's churches. Modern scientific methods are to be used to enable the sending churches to locate these

---

[3] *Ibid.,* p. 34.
[4] *Ibid.*
[5] *Ibid.,* p. 38.
[6] *Ibid.*
[7] *Ibid.,* pp. 39-40

responsive people and great effort is then to be made to send many missionaries to harvest them;[8] not by one-by-one methods but by stimulating a people's movement of whole tribes of communities to church membership.[9]

Some have identified these responsive people with the selectivity of God and have seen a parallel with the history of Israel as Paul has referred to it in Romans 9-11. One such reference is as follows:

> God is selective on the basis of men's response. To those who respond to the light they receive, more light is given. Those who are resistant have that light reduced or taken away . . . . This is the message of Romans 9:11 concerning Israel. A hardening in part had come in Israel and so the light was taken away.[10]

For a brief response to this theology underlying the Church Growth movement—before presenting an alternative theology with its perspective of the place of numbers—the Romans passage is a good place to start. Is it not the position of Paul here that apart from the transforming power of God's call of grace, all men are resistant to Him? In Romans 10:20, Paul quotes Isaiah as saying: "I was found by those who sought me not," referring to the Gentiles. It was not because of their responsiveness God found them. On the contrary, Paul quotes Isaiah further as saying of these Israelites who had apostasized from the true faith by trusting in their own works, "all the day long I have stretched out my hands (the hands of his agents, the prophets) to a disobedient and obstinate people" (Rom. 10:21).

Paul goes on to declare, "God has not rejected his people whom he foreknew" (Rom. 11:2). (Earlier he has identified the foreknown as those predestined to life, Rom. 8:29.) God, he states, had a remnant of 7,000 in Elijah's day:

> In the same way then, there has also come to be at the present time a remnant according to God's gracious choice. But if it is by grace, it is no longer on the basis of works, otherwise grace is no longer grace. What then? That which Israel is seeking for, it has not obtained, but those who were chosen obtained it, and the rest were hardened (Rom. 11:5-7).

---

[8] *Ibid.*, p. 179.
[9] *Ibid.*, pp. 299, 321, 325.
[10] J. Robertson McQuilkin, *Measuring the Church Growth Movement* (Chicago: Moody Press, 1974) p.36.

The responsive seekers of Israel did not get what they wanted, for they were seeking to establish their own righteousness, not God's through Christ (Rom. 10:3,4). But the Gentiles are now receiving it. Why? Because they were responsive, seeking it in Christ? No, they too resisted, satisfied that human effort was adequate (Rom. 3:9-11). All men rejected God but among the rejecting nations as well as among rejecting Israelites, those who obtain God's salvation are a remnant whom He has chosen to save by grace. As Paul points out elsewhere, the curse of death towards God fell on all men in Adam's sin and only by God's gracious supernatural intervention can any be saved. These are those who were chosen before creation.[11]

Our Lord referred to the necessity of this supernatural work as the need for a rebirth by the Spirit (John 3:3 and 5) and went on to declare the selectivity of God involved in one's coming to Christ with these words: "It is the Spirit who gives life .... some of you do not believe..... For this reason I have said to you, that no one can come to Me, unless it has been granted him from the Father" (John 6:63-65). In all of this the fixed nature of the great number God is saving among the nations is far from being contradicted by Christ or His apostles.

Further, far from discouraging a real search for the lost it is the only sound ground for the search. When all men are dead towards God, of what use would it be to go to witness to them if we did not believe God had his elect among them whom He, by supernatural rebirth, would bring to saving faith through His Spirit, in association with the proclamation of His Word (Rom. 10:17)?

The first Protestant Foreign Mission Society was established on this doctrine,[12] one hundred fifty years before William Carey's call, and ever since this time great numbers of Christians have gone to the far corners of the earth in obedience to Christ's command, firmly believing this teaching. In the assurance that God had his elect there and therefore the mission would be as fruitful as it was God's purpose to make it they have searched. This doctrine was not construed to lessen man's responsibility to find the best way possible for the gospel proclamation. These Christians, conforming to Christ's commands and teaching, were and are interested in numbers—God's vast numbers, and their desire has been to be God's agents in reaching those numbers.

---

[11]Romans 5:12-20; Ephesians 2:1-9; 1:4.
[12]Ezra Hoyt Byington, "John Eliot, the Puritan Missionary to the Indians," in *Papers of the American Society of Church History,* ed. by Rev. Samuel Macauley Jackson (New York and London: G. P. Putnam's Sons, The Knickerbocker Press, 1897), pp. 113-118,125.

Why should such searching be identified with "detached witness" and it be said that "mere search is not what God wants"?[13] Is detachment a necessary accompaniment of searching? Why cannot involved people search? (Luke 19:10). What is our calling? Is it to accomplish salvation, or "find" in that sense? We are not the Good Shepherd. He searches and finds. He searches through us, who witness (Acts 1:8). He "finds" through His Spirit, who regenerates. The truly fallen nature of man, and the consequent essentiality of the work of the Spirit in his salvation, do not seem to receive adequate recognition in the theology of missions which defines missions in terms of the missionary's "finding" and "persuading" to eternal life.

Towards a Biblical Theology of Missions

What alternative theology of missions can be proposed? One's understanding of the nature of the church's mission, of the purpose of missions itself, will be reflected in the significance he attaches to the directives of the great commission, Matthew 28:19-20, and to "word and deed" in Romans 15:18. These two passages together present both the aims and methods of missions. There are those who have equated "word" with the biblical gospel and "deed" with the social gospel. Others have thought of word as a spiritual ministry and deed as a physical one. There is a not unbiblical sense in the latter as Romans 15:27 indicates. But can the terms be thought of as exclusive of each other so that one can choose a word ministry and not be responsible for deeds, or vice versa?

A more common recent differentiation is to equate word with proclamation and deed with service. But is not one who proclaims the gospel serving, and are not deeds for Christ a form of Christian proclamation—witness to the love and concern of God? Proclamation by dictionary definition can be verbal or non-verbal, as service can also. Others have suggested that we could consider "word" to mean the evangelistic mandate and "deed" the cultural mandate. But again, can either of these terms or the mandates be thought of as exclusive of each other as if one could consider himself called to engage in one without being involved in the other? The task of missionaries is the proclamation of the gospel; the method must be by word and deed.

Many evangelicals have felt it adequate to state the aim of missions as being the preaching of the gospel for the saving of souls. At the other pole, others have claimed that the missionary's true purpose is to work for social justice and cultural advancement and that such deeds represent the essence

---

[13]McGavran, *op. cit.*, p. 40.

of the proclamation of the gospel. Between these poles many variations exist. To this day this diverse understanding of the nature of our mission confronts us.

As the ultimate purpose of all Christian activity is the glory of God, so the aim of missions must be to accomplish His glory by doing His will in the mission endeavor (John 17:4). His will in this fundamental area of the church's task is clearly enunciated by our Lord in the solemn occasion when, just before He was to return to His glory in heaven, He stood before His apostles, whom He had chosen to be the first officers and builders of His church, and commanded them, and through them all of us, to carry out the stipulations of His new covenant. As Matthew 6:9-13 was given as a model for prayer, so Matthew 28:19-20 has been given as the model for missions. If the church had grasped this concept more thoroughly there doubtless would be today more agreement on the true nature of her mission to the world.

That the prior purpose of the mission is to *make disciples* is clear. This purpose is stated first in the mandate and is an imperative. Until a man becomes a disciple of Christ, he cannot be involved in what follows. To put it another way, until the missionary, the sent one, sees disciples made, he cannot go on to the rest of the task. But the mission does not end with the bringing of men to salvation; rather it only begins there.

The imperative is followed with two participles which also have the force of imperatives by Greek syntax. There is to be *baptizing* of the converts in the Triune name. This is the work of the church's officers, of the institutional church, by which either established churches are enlarged or new ones are planted—an extremely important objective of missions.

But there is a third element in this mission mandate by which our Lord gives to us our model for mission endeavor. The second participle calls for *teaching* the converts all that Christ has commanded. This teaching goes beyond that of the stipulations to make disciples and initiate them into the institutional church. Since the mission was to go out into all the Gentile world, it would be going to people who would have to be taught all that God's Word reveals to us, beginning with the facts of His creation and His mission for men. The mission thus can be defined as the work of the Triune God moving His Church in love to send ambassadors to proclaim the gospel of the kingdom to all the world, by word and deed, to make disciples, build Christ's Church, and teach all His Word for the coming of His kingdom rule in its transforming power upon the individuals, social structures and cultures of the world, for the glory of God.

Covenant Based Theology of Missions

The Westminster Shorter Catechism speaks of the fact that "When God had created man, he entered into a covenant of life with him, before the fall."[14] Traditional Reformed theology has drawn the material for this covenant from Genesis 2 and has spoken of its three or four elements as being the parties, God and man; the condition, perfect obedience; and the penalty and reward, death or continued life. Recent discoveries in the ancient Near East, however, have shown that the covenant form was widely used by the time of Abraham and had a broader structure.[15] Typical suzerainty covenants began with a preamble in which the suzerain was identified, followed by the historical prologue giving the historical situation for the covenantal proclamation. Then came the stipulations, followed by the witnesses, usually deities called to bear witness, and a provision for preserving the remembrance of the covenant. Finally the cursing and blessing formula for disobedience or obedience was stated.

The most characteristic feature of these extra-biblical suzerainty covenants was that the sovereign imposed his will and declared his demands with the vassal accepting in faith and obedience. Is this, too, not the basic feature of the divine covenant concept which underlies all of Scripture as its basic framework? If we draw our material for the covenant of life not only from Genesis 2 but from 1 as well, it seems to me we will see both the full covenant pattern and the answer to the questions as to what is our task and mission in life. In Genesis 1:26-27 God identifies Himself as man's creator. The historical situation is that He has made man to be His image bearer and must now tell him what his mission on earth is to be. The "job description" appears as three stipulations in verse 28: man is to be fruitful and populate the earth; he is to subdue nature; and he is to have dominion over the animal world. In a divine covenant there is no place for deity witnesses, but the tree of the knowledge of good and evil was a constant witness to God's Word concerning the terrible penalty of disobedience, while the tree of life was set as a perpetual remembrance of the covenant of life and its provision for life. The cursing and blessing are stated or implied in 2:17.

---

[14]The Covenant of life phrase comes from Malachi 2:5. Note Hosea 6:7 ASV for reference to the pre-fall covenant.

[15]See G. E. Mendenhall, "Covenant Forms in Israelite Tradition," in a Colloquium reprint from *The Biblical Archaeologist*, Sept. 1954, pp. 26-30. Also J. A. Thompson, *The Ancient Near Eastern Treaties and the Old Testament* (London: The Tyndale Press, 1964).

It is in the stipulations of 1:28, sometimes referred to as the cultural mandate, that we have given to us God's mission for men. Several things should be noted, however. The context of the covenant of life and its stipulations is that man is to render this service for God who is his Lord. Only effort undertaken for God is done in real fulfillment of the covenant of life. Further, the command to reproduce expresses God's concern that men (His image bearers) should produce servants of God to do His bidding and cultivate the world for Him.[16] And finally, the mandate to subdue the earth is a command to bring out the potential of nature, inanimate and animate, and of man himself, to the best of one's ability, for the true advancement of the world and men for the glory of God.

With the fall of mankind into sinful disobedience this covenant of life was not abrogated, however. All men came under its curse provision and lost any desire to fulfill its stipulations for God or to live for His service and glory. If God's purpose, therefore, was not to be frustrated, He must come to them. The merciful introduction after the fall of saving grace, blessed fruit of God's covenant of redemption with His Son, enabled God to renew his covenant of life with men now redeemed and restored to His favor and service—that men should be fruitful, subdue the earth, and have dominion for God. Being fruitful after the fall would mean not only bringing children into the world for God but seeking to bring the children of the world to know God as well (John 15:16). After the fall, being fruitful under the covenant of life, that is, producing servants of God, required redemption and to be its witnesses we are called to this day. The first hint of this new redemptive context to the covenant is given in Genesis 3:15 in the Adamic covenant. Later, in Genesis 17, in the patriarchical age, the Abrahamic administration of the covenant is proclaimed, with its promise of blessing to all the nations of the earth through a Seed-Redeemer and of a world-wide seed as plentiful as the sands of the sea (Genesis 22:17-18). Through Moses, in the national age of God's people, God renewed the covenant, in Deuteronomy and in Exodus 20, presenting ten commandments of stipulations, with blessings and curses, for life under the covenant of life.[17] These were not presented as means for earning life but the way to live a life of grateful obedience. They also revealed to men their hopeless

---

[16]Genesis 2:5 states that God did not have a man to cultivate *(abad)* the ground. *Abad* is translated many times as "serve" which tells us something about the nature of our task.

[17]See Meredith G. Kline, *Treaty of the Great King* (Grand Rapids: Wm. B. Eerdmans Publishing Co., 1963).

imperfection and thus pointed to the need for the perfect obedience of the Redeemer to stand in man's place as covenant keeper.

Finally, with Christ, we come to the new covenant, the final administration of the covenant of life for the international age of the gospel. But where is it in the New Testament? I believe we see it in the great commission, its stipulations appearing in the missionary mandate. The great commission is presented at the end of the Gospels as Christ's last proclamation to His budding church. What is more natural than that, in this final appearance, our Lord should restate His continuing mission for men in terms of the new covenant? In Matthew 28:16-20 we see the basic outline of the typical covenant pattern. The covenant Lord is identified as the risen Jesus who has appointed them to appear before Him. The historical situation is that now all authority has been given Him and He is about to leave them to administer it. The stipulations are that they are to go to make disciples for Him among all peoples, baptizing them into His church and teaching them all He has taught. The witnesses are to be the Holy Spirit-empowered disciples (Acts 1:18), and the constant fellowship of the Lord's Supper is the provision for remembering the Lord and His new covenant (I Corinthians 11:25). The blessing is the promise of His constant presence while the only curse mentioned in connection with the giving of the missionary mandate is the condemnation of those who believe not (Mark 16:16).

Covenant as it has been used here is considered to be an arrangement proclaimed by the sovereign God of love in which He declares His will to His people and binds (obligates) them to Himself with promise during a particular administration of His gracious rule. The stipulations of the first covenant proclamation, with their summary of God's mission to men (Genesis 1:28) clearly inform us of important areas of the teaching we are still enjoined to do by the last covenant proclamation (Matthew 28:19-20). The cultural mandate and the missions mandate are thus vitally related in the ongoing covenant of life. Further, in the latter mandate's stipulation for Christian education, that is, its requirement to teach all that Christ's Word sets forth, His original mission to men is included. The writer of Hebrews in calling attention to our appointed mission (2:7-8) refers to Christ as the one who has come to fulfill it for us. But we are called to be His disciples, to be conformed to His image, to follow Him by endeavoring to bring all things into subjection to Him, through His power, in gratitude to Him. Thus we are called to follow His example by fulfilling the stipulations ourselves for His glory.

Our lives are to be involved in both spiritual and physical ministries. A Christian life involves both dimensions and service to God in both areas. Paul's summary of his missionary activity under the categories of word and deed reveals his concern in both directions (Roman 15:18 and 27). Word and deed seem to be used to summarize his understanding of the method by which the mission his Lord sent him on was to be accomplished. The *evangelistic, ecclesiastical, educational* enterprise was to be the task of the church, but it called for a total commitment of both word and deed. The supreme task of the church in its mission is thus the proclamation of Christ's gospel with a view to the conversion of lost men, the planting and building (spiritually and numerically) of churches with the converts, and the teaching to them of all His Word, by word and deed. Let us consider this further.

Word and Deed Together as Proclamation's Method

Word and deed are both proclamation, for proclamation can be verbal or non-verbal, and the proclamation of the gospel of Christ is the heart of the missionary's mission. The gospel must not be narrowly construed, however. The gospel of Christ is the good news of God's love toward men; of the Father's forgiveness and acceptance by grace; of the Son's redemption from the power, defilement and penalty of sin, received by faith alone; and of the Spirit's empowering for the new life in God's kingdom, restoring to God's fellowship and service forever. Proclaiming this gospel by word is to verbalize the gospel (either by preaching or by witnessing through the spoken and written word) with deeds in harmony with that message of love; proclaiming it by deed is to demonstrate by one's life and acts of compassion the delivering power of the gospel (counteracting the curse through physical help and deeds of mercy) accompanied by verbal testimony in Christ's name. Deeds need words of explanation, and words need deeds of demonstration. In the Old Testament the one word *dabar* can cover both. However, a *dabar* is a word or it can be a deed so eventful that it carries a message in itself. The Bible, however, seldom leaves the deed "word" without verbal interpretation.

To proclaim by word is either preaching or witnessing. Preaching (as the word "herald" implies, II Timothy 4:2) is an official work of the church, an authoritative work (Luke 10:16). Personal, verbal witnessing is a task of every Christian, including the preacher. Both have as objectives fulfilling the three stipulations of the missions mandate and are therefore deeply involved in seeking and urging.

To proclaim by deed is a form of witnessing, the non-verbal form. Jesus said, "The very works that I do, bear witness of me" (John 5:36). Stephen in his death was a silent witness, but he had been a very vocal one. A mere "presence" witness that deliberately omits the name of Christ, on presenting His gospel, cannot be justified. Admittedly the best occasion for the verbal witness is not always easy to recognize and is a matter for prayer and wisdom.

Objectives of the Covenant's Mandate

Under the overall requirement of doing all to the glory of God, the specific objectives, the task, of our verbal witness parallel the stipulations of the new covenant, the mission's mandate to the lost. The first mandate is to go and make disciples. If we take this model for our task seriously, we will be witnessing and preaching for converts—disciples of Christ. This is not the whole task but it starts here if there is to be a forward motion to the next goal. The prayer and deep desire of our hearts must be for the conversion of those to whom we witness. We aim for this, but we know that only God can make anyone into a true disciple of Christ. A disciple in the New Testament terminology is not just one who shows interest in church membership, or even in becoming a Christian, but one who understands to whom he is committing his life and that, although there is much to be gained forever in following Him, there is also a cost to be paid (Luke 14:26, 27, 33). These are not the convictions that come after discipleship has been entered, through a later "perfecting," but are the marks of being made a disciple by the Spirit. Hazardous indeed would it be to accept one for baptism and church membership without these convictions in the hope that through later "perfecting" he would come to them.[18]

In understanding Church Growth much is said about discipling as a first stage and it is differentiated from a second stage of ethical change and dedication to Christ, the goals of the second stage of "perfecting."[19] Four steps are considered as adequate for baptism: (1) first a tribal, corporate rejection of its gods, and fetish burning. (That the tribal deities have been demonstrated to be impotent or non-existent, and the local way of life inferior to that of the missionaries, do not necessarily imply a turning to Christ for salvation, but this fact does not seem to be recognized adequately.) (2) The second step of a tribal corporate acceptance of Christ and enrollment as His people may also be something much short of

---

[18]McGavran, *op. cit.*, p. 315.
[19]McGavran, *The Bridges of God* (London: World Dominion Press, 1961), p.15.

personal repentance and faith. (3) The next steps of choosing leaders and (4) attending regular church services likewise do not necessarily indicate saving faith. Many unregenerate people could be involved in this corporate movement. How then can it be said that those that do these things are disciples, and that "It would be equally sinful and foolish to refuse baptism to groups who are prepared to carry out the four steps mentioned above..."?[20] Baptism and church membership for people who may not have made a personal faith commitment to Christ for salvation[21] will indeed increase church statistics—numbers—but do they really represent church growth? The question may well be asked, "What implications do we predispose ourselves towards, or to what kind of presuppositions have we already committed ourselves, if we divide the experiences of becoming a Christian into two distinct segments, one of which is minimal while the other moves on towards perfection."[22]

The second objective is stated in terms of "baptizing" the disciples. This is an ecclesiastical task, the initiatory rite into membership in a church organization, a sign of membership in the body of Christ. It is administered by a church officer and is a step toward planting a new church or expanding an existing one. But this church growth is not the whole task, nor the whole goal. As the place of the first aim of making disciples, in its conversion aspect, was prior so this one of church growth is central to the missions task.

Adult baptism, followed by a church membership which entitles one to share in the table of the Lord, is a highly personal matter. It is the individual's witness to the world that he has truly broken with the sins of his past and identified himself with Jesus Christ by faith, regardless of the cost—that he has indeed "turned to God from idols to serve the living and true God and to wait for His Son from heaven whom He raised from the dead, that is Jesus, who delivers us from the wrath to come" (I Thessalonians 1:9-10). This is church growth that is spiritual and numerical, the growth that is at the very heart of missions.

---

[20]McGavran, *Understanding Church Growth,* p. 315.

[21]Donald G. McGavran, "Church Growth Strategy Continued" in *Eye of the Storm, the Great Debate in Mission,* ed. by McGavran (Waco: Word Boods, Publisher, 1972), p. 178. Note the sequence in the following statement: "they do not require the baptism of bodies, the salvation of souls, and the building of visible new churches."

[22]John H. Yoder, "Church Growth Issue in Theological Perspective," in *The Challenge of Church Growth,* a symposium ed. by Wilbert R. Shenk (Elkhart, Ind.: Institute of Mennonite Studies, 1973), pp. 33-34.

Can a mass people's movement be reflective of this? History is replete with illustrations of such movements with minimal discipling building shallow churches, with faith becoming syncretistic and then dying away. From the Constantinian movement, to the mass conversions of the central plains of Asia, the tribes of the Kerites, Onguss, and Uigars,[23] to the Roman Catholic conversions of southern Japan[24] such illustrations exist.

The Dani of West New Guinea in the past two decades have seen remarkable numbers of their people converted. McGavran points out that their movement to burn their fetishes was spontaneous and massive.[25] Some missionaries at first opposed the burning, which has started under the pressure of a Roman Catholic priest, on the grounds that the people thought they could obtain eternal life, never dying on earth, by that means.[26] But "Fortunately the Dani knew what they were going to do!" and continued to burn their charms, it is stated.[27]

S. Horne relates what some missionaries did in another area[28] after the burning:

> Thousands of confessed "converts" could have been baptized immediately following the fetish burning. This could have resulted only in many falling away. A solid church grounded in knowledge of the scriptures was the objective of the mission. Therefore, with so much counterfeit mingled with the genuine, no one was baptized until his life evidenced that he both understood and acted upon the principles of the Christian faith.

> Out of the thousands turning to Christ, only eight Danis were baptized at Kelila on Sunday, July 29, 1962 . . . .[29]

---

[23]Christopher Dawson, *Mission to Asia* (New York: Harper and Row, Publishers, 1955), p. 325. See also John Stewart, *Nestorian Missionary Enterprise* (Edinburgh: T. & T. Clark, 1928), pp. 138-168.

[24]John M. L. Young, *The Two Empires in Japan* (Philadelphia: Presbyterian and Reformed Publishing Co., 1961), pp. 9-24.

[25]McGavran, *Understanding Church Growth p. 152.*

[26]Shirley Horne, *An Hour to the Stone Age* (Chicago: Moody Press, 1973), p.126.

[27]McGavran, *op. cit.,* pp. 152-153.

[28]Unevangelized Fields Mission area. Other missions were working in the neighboring area to which McGavran refers in his quotations from James Sunda, *Church Growth in West New Guinea* (Lucknow: Lucknow Publishing House, 1963).

[29]Horne, *op. cit.,* p. 160.

Horne further states:

> Out of the great mass movement, individuals have come to make a personal accounting with God. In each area forty to fifty were baptized each month.)[30]

This seems much more in keeping with the biblical concept of discipling and the meaning of baptism. Corporate voting to burn fetishes and corporate voting to become "Christians" were not considered adequate grounds to be included in the number of the church by this mission.[31] Both some knowledge of the basis of the Christian faith and some practice that evidences a yielding to the rule of Christ were asked for—and the church grew. Even as Luke wrote: "And the Lord added to the church daily such as should be saved" (Acts 2:47).

The final stipulation, as set forth in the mission model, is the requirement for teaching—Christian education. Christian education must take place in the home, the church, the church school, and where possible, in Christian day schools. All of Christ's instruction, all his Word, with its implications for life in our world, needs presentation with an emphasis to the youth that all of this life must be sacred, though lived for God in a pagan or secularized society.

Christian education is for Christian students, by means of which a Christian perspective of cultural, social, and ethical problems for life in God's world can be obtained. Teaching in such a context should not have to become primarily an evangelistic effort. Christian schools which have opened their doors to large numbers of non-Christians have found it difficult to maintain both evangelism and Christian education successfully. Christian education is of exceptional importance for the training of a strong leadership for church and community. Christians and their churches must be taught to think of Christian schools as a common effort, requiring their communal support for the sound growth of their church and the advancement of God's kingdom.

The model of an evangelistic, ecclesiastical, and educational program is the one our Lord has set before us for the church's mission, all three being objectives of the church's mission task, while the method is by word and deed, through the empowering of the Spirit and the constraining love of Christ. Mission agencies will do well to take this model for their frame of reference in their mission task.

---

[30] *Ibid.*, pp. 162-163.
[31] *Ibid.*, pp. 127-129.

The Importance of Numbers

In conclusion, it is necessary to say something more about the importance of numerical growth. We have considered the place of such growth as we examined the theological promises behind the rejection of "search theology" and promotion of "harvest theology," by the founder of the Church Growth movement, and found it lacking an adequately biblical perspective. We have also found lacking its methodology stemming from these premises—one of seeking out a "responsive people" among pagan people, endeavoring to maneuver them into a corporate "people's movement," considering them "disciples" if they corporately voted for fetish burning and for becoming "Christians," and baptizing them into church membership.[32] The emphasis on rapid church growth by increase of numbers along these lines may increase the size and number of congregations, but does it contribute to a corresponding increase in the redeemed body of Christ?

We have also endeavored to set forth a biblically grounded theology of missions based on a larger view of the covenant concept, one within the Reformed framework but extending beyond its traditional scope in structure and content, one giving the church a model for its task in this international age of the covenant.

Numbers in the context of this theology are related to the promise of the Father to the Son in the covenant of redemption—that all whom the Father ordained to eternal life (Acts 13:48) He would give to the Son who would certainly save them (John 6:37,44). On the basis of this covenanted redemption, God could covenant with Abraham to "greatly multiply your seed as the stars of the heaven and the sand of the seashore;" and could promise "in your seed all the nations of the earth shall be blessed" (Genesis 22:17-18; note Galatians 3:29).

These are the ones Christ purchased for God with His blood, men "from every tribe and tongue and people and nation" (Revelations 5:9), a number fixed before creation (Ephesians 1:4) whom God alone saves. His church, however, has the privilege of the great task of sending out His ambassadors to take His saving gospel to them. God is indeed interested in numbers, His numbers, and in their addition to His churches.

---

[32]See articles by James A. Scherer, "The Life and Growth of Churches in Mission," in *Mission Trends No. 1* (Grand Rapids: Wm. B. Eerdmans Publishing Co., 1974), pp. 165-177: and *The Challenge of Church Growth*, symposium ed. by W. R. Shenk, *op. cit.*

But the goal of added numbers must not be absolutized. They are not the only valid measurement of church growth. The response of churches to the total covenant task of the evangelistic, ecclesiastical, and educational stipulations of Christ is a far more complete biblical criterion for evaluation of church growth. What are the churches doing about seeking the lost? Is this a vital concern to them? Are they bringing the converts into existing churches, and planting new churches in homes or communal buildings where they are lacking? Are they teaching them how to live in the world, how to influence their society and culture for God, how to witness the gospel in word and deed, teaching all Christ's Word? Are they seeking to fulfill the stipulations required of His people that Christ may build His church and add those ordained to life? For man's salvation Christ calls upon us to do what we can do in obedience to His will and to trust Him to do what we cannot. Such criteria will furnish material for valid evaluation of a church's growth where mere numbers cannot. The strength of a church is not just in its numbers.

God wants His church to grow. This means the churches should be growing. Paul speaks of himself as a builder, but adds, "God causes the growth" (I Corinthians 3:7-10). Church growth is implied in what he is saying. But it must be on the foundation of Jesus Christ. Lowering the standards for membership and baptism to "a minimal" basis so all in a tribe can accept them, and thus tribal opposition to becoming "Christians" be changed to putting pressure on all to assent to a "people's movement," may get great numbers, the whole tribe in fact, but what then is their personal relation to Jesus Christ? Have they been brought by a strategy or by the convicting power of the Holy Spirit? Have they substituted new rites for old with their faith still in externals and their sense of security still basically in their tribal identity? If personal confidence in Christ is lacking in an individual, what does baptism mean to him? The Lord's count excludes those who come to Him without committing all to Him and the desire to do His will, even to being willing to break with kin in order to be His disciple (Matthew 7:21-23; Luke 14:26).

Without the pressure of a personal decision, and acting only in the traditional corporate way, will not Christ be left at the periphery of life and the tribe still be at the center? Will not the very ease of the corporate decision and the steps to baptism remove from both any thought of a radical break with the faith which put all hope of security and salvation in identity with the tribe and its teaching? If at baptism there is lacking the awareness of personally deciding to stand with Christ, and of putting all hope in Him for life on earth and life eternal, on what foundation are they still standing? Does such baptism and church membership advance church growth or hinder it?

The foundation for church growth is Jesus Christ. God who causes the growth builds on that foundation. His eternal purpose includes the total number He will save, a great number fixed before creation. The certainty of the existence of such a number is a great incentive to search for them. The knowledge that they must be saved through the church fulfilling its mission of working with Christ to build His church is a great incentive to work at the building. The awareness that God's eternal purpose includes the plan, the covenanted model, for the growth of the church through the incorporation of this number, is a great incentive to follow the plan. Above all, our love for God and for our fellow men is a great incentive to share that love with them for His glory. It is God's decree that this number be reached. That is how important numerical church growth is.

CHAPTER FIVE

WHAT ARE PEOPLE MOVEMENTS?

by Robert Recker*

If we are to speak of people movements, we must answer the question, what is a people? Webster defines a people as follows:

> A body of persons united by a common character, culture, or sentiment; the individuals collectively of any characteristic group, conceived apart from the unity of the group as subject to a common government (that is, as a *state*) or as issued from a common stock (that is, as a *race* or tribe).[1]

This definition is sufficient for us to move on in using the rather vague term "people" in this paper.

At an early point in the development of the "Church Growth" emphasis, Dr. Donald McGavran defined the term a bit more specifically, writing:

> Basic to the entire point of view is the concept of a people. A people is a society whose members marry exclusively within it. Whether such a caste or tribe is really racially distinct from others is immaterial. As long as its sons take wives only from the people itself, so long will it think of itself as a really separate race and will have an intense "people

---

Robert Recker is Professor of Missions at Calvin Theological Seminary, Grand Rapids, Michigan. From 1950 to 1965, he served with the Christian Reformed Church in Nigeria where his work among the Hausa people there involved him in church planting, instruction of pastors, and production of basic educational literature. He has been at Calvin Seminary since 1969.

---

[1] *Webster's Collegiate Dictionary* (Fifth Edition; Springfield, Mass.: G. & C. Merriam Co., Publishers, 1946)

consciousness." Its intimate life will be restricted to itself. Clan loyalty or people loyalty will be the highest virtue.[2]

Immediately we are faced with the question as to the value which we place upon such ethnic groupings. Do we view peoplehood as a creational given or do we see it as an ephemeral, historical, social development? This is very important, for it will determine the importance we attach to the social unit.

This has been lastingly illustrated in the position of Bruno Gutmann who served the Leipzig Mission as missionary among the Chagga people of the Kilimanjaro region from 1902 to 1938.[3] He saw man not primarily as an individual but as "a member of an organic social unit."[4] To understand man one must see him "in, through and for the community."[5] He viewed such social units as creation ordinances, and hence, in effect, as expressions of the Word and will of God. This would inevitably lead to a close tie-in of the structure of the church with the structure of the people. Certainly the church would be called upon to respect and not to disrupt or destroy the creational givens, if these social groupings are not in any way the product of man's sinful tendency to divisions.[6] The best approach on the part of the mission would then be an organic approach to the whole people, and one that presupposes an inter-relation between church and peoplehood. Hence Gutmann could say:

> Both the Church and fundamental human ties are created by God and are dependent upon each other and thus represent God's immanent Being in the world of men.[7]

Such a high evaluation of the social-ethnological groupings of men would definitely affect the manner of gospel-approach not only, but also of

---

[2]J. W. Pickett, A. L. Warshuis, G. H. Singh, D. A. McGavran, *Church Growth and Group Conversion,* (Lucknow, U.P., India: Lucknow Publishing House, 1956, p. 5. Cf. Mc Gavran, D. A., *Understanding Church Growth* 1936, Grand Rapids, Mich.: Eerdmans, '70, pp. 296-299.

[3] *Concise Dictionary of the Christian World Mission,* edited by Stephen Neill, Gerald H. Anderson, John Goodwin, (Nashville and New York: Abingdon Press, 1971), p. 239.

[4]Peter Beyerhaus and Henry Lefever, *The Responsible Church and the Foreign Mission* (London: World Dominion Press, 1964), p.50

[5]*Ibid.*

[6] *Concise Dictionary of the Christian World Mission, op. cit.,* p. 239.

[7]Beyerhaus and Lefever, *op. cit.,* pp. 50-51.

the later make-up of the church which would emerge. Beyerhaus is right in calling attention to another factor which would influence the nature of missionary approach to such groupings, namely, the understanding of how the Word of God operates.[8] How does a man hear and respond to the proclaimed Word of God, how does he come to a decision as confronted by the living God through His Word, and how does he express that decision which has crystallized in his heart as effectuated by the very Spirit of God? We will not go into this point, even though it is very important, except to remark that this is illustrated by the Church Growth school's calling attention to the communal nature of decision-making among many peoples.[9]

To simplify the discussion I would like to propound that there are only three creational givens: the individual, the family, and the race. I would contend that peoplehood is an historical development which is subject to change, and not to be viewed as ultimate in any sense. Certain representatives of South African *apartheid* politics illustrate the consequences of viewing these ethnological divisions as creational givens and hence as expressions of the will of God which not only must be respected but also guarded.

Dr. Harry Boer has called attention to the significance of the family unit in the outreach of the Christian church from its earliest beginnings.[10] McGavran has eloquently called us to discern the very "bridges of God" in the web or relationships provided by the "extended family."[11] This web is where the most intimate of relationships take place and provide the natural avenues for the spontaneous witnessing of Christians in their immediate environment, addressed to those who are most vulnerable to that witness, and who are best able to judge the quality of the Christian life of the one

---

[8] *Ibid.,* p.51.

[9] Donald A. McGavran, *Understanding Church Growth* (Grand Rapids, Michigan: William B. Eerdmans Publishing Company, 1970), pp. 302-304. J. Waskom Pickett, *The Dynamics of Church Growth* (New York - Nashville: Abingdon Press, 1963), pp. 24-25.

[10] Harry R. Boer, *Pentecost and Missions* (Grand Rapids, Michigan: Wm. B. Eerdmans Publishing Co., 1961), pp. 165-185.

[11] D. A. Mc Gavran, *The Bridges of God. A Study in the Strategy of Missions* (New York: Friendship Press, 1968, 1955, pp. 17-35, 71. D. A. Mc Gavran with Win C. Arn, *How to Grow a Church* (Glendale, California: A Division of G/L Publications, 1973), pp. 32-34. Mc Gavran, *Understanding Church Growth,* pp. 320-325.

who witnesses. Hence one can speak of the hope for the spontaneous expansion of the Christian church.[12]

It appears to me that J. W. Pickettt, Donald McGavran and others are working with the "people" concept as an extension of the family, as an extension of the grid of a family and its relatives. Yet they see the bulk of the action taking place in the familial context which can then be extended to clan and beyond. The acme of the process is that moment when upper segregated castes are provoked to jealousy by despised lower castes to seek the same life-empowering and uplifting secret![13]

In addressing the concept of "nation" or "people," we must remember that biblically this is often to be seen as those peoples who are contrasted to "the people of God" and not primarily in their ethnic sense.[14] Such peoples are to be seen in the light of Ephesians, chapter two, as alienated from God, as those who are at a distance from the divine action which has been taking place in the midst of a particular people. This is then descriptive of their emptiness, of their need. But they are also depicted in the Scripture as the observers of the divine action in and concerning the Israel of God. Furthermore, they are to be seen as the arena in which God's great legal confrontation with fallen man takes place. But even more, this complex of peoples is seen as the gift of God to His Messiah over whom He is to reign, and whom He is to subjugate by the twofold cutting edge of His word.[15]

We must remember that no matter how transitory one would view the phenomenon of peoplehood, the gospel of Jesus Christ is addressed to and finds people where they are. It addresses flesh and blood people who are

---

[12]D. T. Niles, *Upon The Earth. The Mission of God and the Missionary Enterprise of the Churches* (New York - Toronto - London: McGraw-Hill Book Company, Inc., 1962), p. 204. Roland Allen, *The Spontaneous Expansion of the Church* (London: 1949, Second Edition) (World Dominion Press, 1927).

[13]J. Waskom Pickett, *Christ's Way to India's Heart* (Lucknow: W. W. Bell, 1960 /*1938*/ pp. 41-43.

[14]"When the term   is used in the sense of Gentiles, it is often with no sense of a plurality of nations. The word is used non-sociologically to describe all the individuals who do not belong to the chosen people." Cf. George Bertram, ἔϑνος ἐϑνικός *Theological Dictionary of the New Testament* Vol. II, Edited by Gerhard Kittel, Translator and Editor, Geoffrey W. Bromiley, (Grand Rapids, Michigan: Wm. B. Eerdmans Publishing Company, 1964), p. 367. Cf. also Johannes Blauw, *The Missionary Nature of the Church. A Survey of the Biblical Theology of Mission* (New York - Toronto - London: McGraw-Hill Book Company, Inc., 1962), pp. 25-37.

[15]Psalm 2, 110; Isaiah 49:5-7, 22, 26; 55:4-5, 11; 59:15-21; 60:1-5, 10-12, 16; Hag. 2:7; Zech. 9:9-10; 14:9; Mal. 3:1-12; Revelation 5:13; 6:2; 19:11-16; 21:24-27.

more or less communally oriented and who function more or less in communal fashion. There can be no docetism here. The royal proclamation of the risen, victorious, exalted and reigning Lord directs his subjects to go out and to disciple people who live in complexes of peoplehood. The gospel speaks to and is opposite to the situation of the man where he is; the living Lord confronts men as they live in community.

It is thus very important to note carefully that the Church Growth school is speaking of the manner or method of approach and not about the on-going nature or make-up of an ethnic or national church. The role of the church in the nation and as an expression of the nation in the kingdom of God is a much more difficult problem. A number of Dutch theologians have developed this relation of the church to national life, and as a representative of the churches in developing lands. D. T. Niles would carry this matter beyond the simple question of approach. He recognizes the importance of the approach question in the words, "The missionary movement of the Church must reckon with nationhood in the world."[16] Yet he also speaks a word of caution:

> Where caution is expressed against attempting to identify "the nations" in the Bible with the modern nation-states, that caution must be needed; for it is so easy to slip from a concern to build a church for the nation into a desire to build a church of the nation.[17]

Recognizing the importance of distinguishing between the matter of missionary approach and that of the nature of the church which comes into being by means of missionary outreach, there remains one point of issue. A number of men in seeking biblically to ground the accent on seeking people's movements, seek grounds for this in the book of Acts.[18] It is true that the early New Testament church was in the main Jews or former Jewish proselytes or God-fearers; in that sense they were a definable social group and the synagogue provided a bridge and arena for the church's early expansion. Nevertheless, this does not provide a good parallel nor a biblical basis for the later peoples movements.

---

[16]Niles, *op. cit.,* p. 256; also the entire section: "The World of Nations — The Secular Frontier," pp. 247-270.

[17] *Ibid.,* p. 255. Pickett, *The Dynamics of Church Growth,* pp. 107-124.

[18]Mc Gavran, *The Bridges of God,* pp. 17-35. Picket, *op. cit.,* pp. 11-16. A. R. Tippett, *Church Growth and the Word of God. The Biblical Basis of the Church Growth Viewpoint* (Grand Rapids, Michigan: William B. Eerdmans Publishing Company, 1970), pp. 28-33, 23.

Pickett and McGavran rightly like to speak of the "transfer of loyalties" which is the heart of conversion whether it be of the individual or of the individual in community.[19] But this cannot so easily be said of the early New Testament converts. They were moving from an Old Testament Faith in Yahweh which looked forward to the coming of His Messiah to the New Testament faith which recognized and accepted the Messiah of Yahweh as one who has already come. This was a transitional period in which the Messiah indeed was demonstrated as the glory of Israel, and as the one who, sent by God, revitalized the life and faith of the historic people of Yahweh. This was his first task according to the Isaianic servant songs, and this was why in his own public ministry he was sent to the household of Israel. Only in and through this stage of his ministry would the second stage be effected, namely that he would become the light to the Gentiles. This period in the early life of the church along with the synagogal context would never be reduplicated in the history of the expansion of the Christian church. But when one challenges a man who serves another so-called god to turn to the living God (I Thessalonians 1), that is truly a call for a transfer of loyalties. In our appeal to scripture we must be careful lest we oversimplify matters and see parallels where there is not really a parallel.

This brings us to our second main question, What is a people movement? It is interesting in the literature to see the shift in terminology from "mass movements," to "group conversion," to "people movement," to "multi-individual conversion," to "multi-individual interdependent decision."[20] McGavran can speak of a "mass transfer of loyalties,"[21] and in accord with this A. L. Warshuis indicates the simple heart of what is at stake here as expressed in the short biblical confession: "Jesus is Lord!"[22] He goes on to guard against any setting up of an individual/communal dichotomy:

---

[19]Mc Gavran, *op. cit.,* pp. 38-40, 14. J. Waskom Pickett, *Christian Mass Movements in India. A Study With Recommendations* (New York - Cincinnati - Chicago: The Abingdon Press, 1933), p. 23.

[20]Pickett et alia, *Church Growth and Group Conversion,* pp. 1-6. Pickett, *Christian Mass Movements in India,* pp. 21-26. McGavran, *Understanding Church Growth,* pp. 302-304. Alan R. Tippett, "The Holy Spirit and Responsive Populations," *Crucial Issues in Missions Tomorrow,* Edited by Donald A. McGavran, (Chicago: Moody Press, 1972), pp. 77-79. Mc Gavran, *The Bridges of God,* p. 13. J. Robertson McQuilkin, *Measuring The Church Growth Movement How Biblical Is It?* (Chicago: Moody Press, 1973-1974), p. 45

[21]McGavran, *op. cit.,* pp. 38-40.

[22]Pickett et alia, *op. cit.,* p. 17.

To a large extent, all religious work is with individuals. In group conversion, the individual is still as important as ever. Groups are influenced through individuals. The mistake occurs when the objective is only the individual who is separated from the group. Instead of separating him from the group, the individual should lead the way into the group.[23]

We can thus conclude that we are speaking of a multiple shift of people from one religious allegiance to another, and that this transfer of loyalties takes place not one by one but in concert. There is a symphonic movement to Christ in the midst of a definable people rather than a solo movement. The individual makes this decision about the ultimate in community and not as separate from that community. He makes this decision with the support of his peers and not in antithetical relation to his peers. This seems to be a key point in the development of this church growth thinking in the context of the situation in India. It also ties in with another key consideration of Pickett, McGavran, and others, namely, that the new convert remains in relation with his natural web of relatives and contacts, and not be extracted from this web into some "called out" "gathered colony."[24]

But there are many multiple conversions which cannot be classed as a "people movement." McGavran ventures the figure of a 50% or more rate of growth per decade as indicative of the presence of a people movement. He reckons on a normal growth rate of 15% as simply the increase of births over deaths, and that would leave a 35% rate of growth from the non-Christian population. He then goes on to say:

A People Movement could scarcely grow less without being arrested. It should normally grow more. The norm of 50 per cent per decade is based on a study of the growth of these movements, and it is a workable figure which will serve meanwhile.[25]

One of the reasons for the great interest in the matter of a "mass transfer of loyalties" is the fact that this immediately provides a community for the convert, a fellowship circle which is not on the periphery of the culture.

---

[23] *Ibid.,* p. 18.
[24] Mc Gavran, *op. cit.,* pp. 46-48, 100-108. Pickett, *Christ's Way to India's Heart,* pp. 86-88.
[25] *Ibid.,* p. 113.

Hence there is no isolation of and resulting stagnation of the movement. It is not branded as anti-community![26] So a living involvement in society is carried on, and an increasing penetration of that strata of the population is a possiblity.

One does not have to read very far in this literature to note that a high estimate is placed on group ingathering for the expansion of Christianity. Pickett makes the following remarks:

> Mass Movements, induced by group decision, have been common throughout Christian history and it is not clear that any race or nation has ever been brought to Christian faith except by mass movements.[27]

Again he states:

> To the mind of the writer the conclusion is inescapable that Christ is moving into the heart of India not along the lonely road of the detached individual but through the crowded thoroughfares of community life.[28]

A. L. Warshuis makes a more radical judgment in this regard:

> The propagation of religion from one community or land to another has never been accomplished by detaching individuals from their social groupings. Men never do anything of importance except in groups, and religion has been propagated only by group movements.[29]

McGavran expresses similar sentiments:

> The power of God acts best within a people. Christianity has flowed most powerfully when it has flowed within peoples.[30]

> God has been discipling the peoples. For every one out of a new people brought to Christian faith from his group, God has converted hundreds in chains of families. He has used the People Movement. That is the normal way in which the Christian churches have grown.[31]

McGavran is one with Pickett in reading the pages of Christian history:

---

[26]Pickett, *The Dynamics of Church Growth*, pp. 23-24.
[27]Pickett, *Christ's Way to India's Heart*, p. 28. McGavran, *op. cit.*, pp. 107-108.
[28]Pickett, *op. cit.*, p. 32; also cf. pp. 83-84.
[29]Pickett et alia, *Church Growth and Group Conversion*, p. 11.
[30]McGavran, *op. cit.*, pp. 93-94.
[31]*Ibid.*, pp. 107-108.

The story is too well known to need recapitulation. We merely call attention to it. Christendom arose out of *People Movements*. The only continent where most of the population became even nominally Christian was the continent which was won for Christ in a long series of People Movements![32]

These statements not only reveal a certain reading of the history of the expansion of the Christian church, but they also reveal a very strong accent on the communal aspect of the nature of man. As Stephen Neill observes, this kind of advance has taken place mainly among people on the "animistic level."[33] The yellow races are not as readily seen in this reading of Christian history.[34]

There are three factors which make us pause before we would designate "people movement operation" as normative mission procedure in order to win the remaining 2,700,000,000 to Christ. Or we might phrase the question thus: Is this the way not only into India's heart, but also into the world's heart?[35]

(1) McGavran himself is not bashful in declaring that "It is a God-designed pattern by which not ones but thousands will acknowledge Christ as Lord, and grow into full discipleship as people after people, clan after clan, tribe after tribe, and community after community are claimed for and nurtured in the Christian faith."[36]

Yet McGavran honestly calls attention to the inexplicable or mysterious in these movements.

Yet we not only affirm it, but go further and claim that the vast stirrings of the Spirit which occur in people movements are God-given. We dare not think of people movements to Christ as merely social phenomena. True, we can account for some of the contributing factors which have brought them about; but there is so much that is mysterious and beyond anything we can ask or think, so much that is a product of religious faith, and so much evident working of divine

[32] *Ibid.,* p. 38.
[33] *Concise Dictionary of the Christian World Missions p. 111.*
[32]Stephen Neill, *A History of Christian Missions* Middlesex: Peguin Books, 1964), p. 327. Donald A. McGavran, *How Churches Grow. The New Frontiers of Mission* (London: World Dominion Press, 1959), pp. 123-124.
[35]Pickett, *The Dynamics of Church Growth,* p. 26.
[36]McGavran, *The Bridges of God,* p. 67.

power, that we must confess that people movements are gifts of God.[37]

We therefore have a complication in setting up our mission procedure in that God works where He wills. McGavran also calls attention to the obtuseness and disobedience of men in this relation.

> One of the curious facts about People Movements is that they have seldom been sought or desired. Pickett records, in *Christian Mass Movements in India,* that most People Movements have actually been resisted by the leaders of the church and mission where they started.[38]

How does McGavran react to this uncontrollable factor in church growth? He simply states,

> Yes, we should concentrate where God has ripened the field. When we find people in need, we should minister the Gospel. People do not become ripe by accident. They ripen by the purpose of God. It is true that various factors play upon them, but who produces the factors? The church is well advised to consider that responsiveness means the finger of God pointing at that population saying, "Go and bear witness there. A church is waiting to be born."[39]

John T. Seamands simply states, "We must work where the Holy Spirit is working."[40]

All one can say to this from biblical perspective is "Amen!" In actual practice it gradually leads to a mission policy of moving in and assisting movements which are already in progress. There then follows the Church Growth school's accent on priorities, concentration of resources where there is fruit or harvest, and a corresponding call for mobility (not to get tied down in a mission station or in costly institutions unless they really nurture a people movement).

---

[37]*Ibid.,* p. 81; cf. also pp. 93-94, 107-108. *God, Man and Church Growth. A Festschrift in Honor of Donald Anderson McGavran,* Edited by A. R. Tippett, (Grand Rapids, Michigan: Wm. B. Eerdmans Publishing Co., 1973), p. 105.

[38]McGavran, *op. cit.,* pp. 80 - 81.

[39]McGavran and Arn, *How To Grow A Church,* p. 56.

[40]John T. Seamands, "The Role of the Holy Spirit in Church Growth," *God, Man and Church Growth,* p. 106; cf. also p. 57. Tippett, *Crucial Issues In Missions Tomorrow,* pp. 77-101. McGavran, *How Churches Grow,* p. 58.

In one sense this is simple recognition of the truth that God through His Spirit prepares the soil.[41] He is the Lord of the harvest, and hence areas differ as to the quality and the intensity of the response.[42] Hence, one of the most basically biblical answers to the question, What are people movements?, is simply this: they are the gift of God, they are the product of His gracious activity, and they can be explained in no other way.

On the other hand, however, the Church Growth school would emphasize the human responsibility aspects of this matter and so they call for a fierce pragmatism. The two accents are brought together in that they call for a "pragmatism which is Spirit-directed and Spirit-filled."[43] The Church Growth school's accent on planting churches (congregations) expresses a goal of pragmatic strategy.[44]

(2) The second factor which must be considered is really a correlate of the first. That is the concept of the *kairoi* or open doors which are provided by the Spirit of God in the varied and changing fabric of human society. McGavran calls attention to the fact that pure animists are on the move, they are changing their religious allegiance, and this process will take forty to fifty years.[45] This is a very important observation, and I can only concur on the basis of what has happened among the smaller tribes of northern Nigeria in the last fifty years. Open doors do not remain open, whether that be a door to a village or to a family or to a tribe. And it is the lasting sadness of many a missionary to remember open doors of the past which were not passed through quickly enough. But this matter of "open doors," of the "opportune time," cannot be controlled nor produced at will. Yet it is possible to pray God for such *kairoi* of the Spirit, and it is incumbent on us to respond with alacrity when we suddenly stand before an open door! Hence at times we must wait, pray, watch, and fast in discomfort![46]

(3) This leads us to one aspect of the preceding point, namely, that there are epochs, great transitional periods in history which will never be repeated. They are once-for-all periods during which many of the historic people

---

[41] *God, Man and Church Growth*, pp. 154, 104-107.

[42] *Ibid.*, p. 154. McGavran, *op. cit.*, pp. 2, 129.

[43] *God, Man and Church Growth*, pp. 148.

[44] *Ibid.*, pp. 157, 146-158. McGavran, *op. cit.*, pp. 122-131. McGavran and Arn, *How to Grow a Church*, p. 169.

[45] McGavran, *How Churches Grow*, pp. 48-49, 129-130. Mc Gavran, *The Bridges of God*, p. 15, 90.

[46] McGavran, *How Churches Grow*, p. 130.

movements have taken place. This too is a factor which is out of our control, but the Lord of history who shakes up the peoples is still able to convince great groups of people that they have gone down an historical blind alley, leading them to look for another alternative. And prayer is the incense which God co-opts in His Messianic-mediated rule in this eon.[47] But is the desire there, and hence the prayer?[48]

Granted that minimal desire is present in the church and in the Christian community, the least that can be asked of us is that we study people movements which have taken place, that we rejoice in and praise God for those that are presently taking place, and that we beseech God in His grace to inspire new movements to the Christ worldwide. For us in the west this means that we gain a new appreciation for the communal side of man's nature, and that we structure our congregational life and our liturgical activities so that there is more room for its expression.

This brings us to our third main section in answering the question, What are people movements? Simply put, we must name some of the historic incidences of this phenomenon. As far as Roman Catholicism is concerned we recall the movement of the fisher folk around Cape Comorin and Ramnad, the movement in Chota Nagpur, and the movement in Japan between 1565 and 1575. Stephen Neill calls attention to the first Protestant mass movement in India between 1795 and 1805 in the midst of the illiterate Nadar (Shanar) community.[49] J. Waskom Pickett places the significant year as 1817-1818, when three thousand Nadars were gathered in.[50] "Between 1875 and 1879 nearly 9,000 persons became Christians."[51] There are also the Chuhra movement of the Sialkot District, the Anglican-Lutheran movements of Chota Nagpur and Assam, the movement of the Madigas and others in Telugu country, the sweeper movement in the United Provinces,[52] the Andhra Desa movement which has jumped several caste lines,[53] the movement among the Ooriya Garas,[54] the Santals, and others. Looking farther afield we think of the Karens, the Bataks, the movement in Korea, the movement among the mountain tribes of Taiwan,

---

[47]Revelation 8:3-4.
[48]McGavran, *op. cit.,* pp. 127-128.
[49]Neill, *op. cit.,* p. 235.
[50]Pickett, *Christian Mass Movements in India,* p. 41.
[51] *Ibid.,* p. 42.
[52] *Ibid.,* pp. 51-52.
[53]Pickett, *Christ's Way to India's Heart,* pp. 60 ff.
[54]Pickett et alia, *Church Growth and Group Conversion,* pp. 21-35.

the early growth under persecution in Madagascar,[55] the wildfire growth in Ethiopia, Catholic-Protestant growth in Buganda, movements among the Ibo, Yoruba, and Tiv in Nigeria, movements in Brazil, Chile, Colombia, and the Naranjo people movement in Argentina, movements in Chiapas-Oaxaca areas of Mexico, and many more. Where does one begin? I can only call attention to a couple of them.

Raymond J. Davis has dramatically told the story of the Wallamo people movement of southwestern Ethiopia.[56] Here is an instance of 48 converts multiplying to 10,000 in five years while the missionaries were withdrawn and while Ethiopia was under foreign occupation. In his preface, author Davis states:

> To the questions, Why did all this happen in Wallamo? Why did God choose to do this wonderful thing here? the ultimate answer is a mystery. The phenomenal growth of the church and the effectiveness of the Gospel in Wallamo can only be attributed to the work of the Holy Spirit. What happened in Wallamo could never have been produced by human effort, however devoted.[57]

This is that mysterious uncontrollable factor concerning which we have spoken and which is recognized by representatives of the Church Growth school.[58]

In striking contrast to this are those people movements which under God have been triggered by the key personality. Ed Murphy has given us an interesting summary of the Victor Landero people movement (San Jorge-Cauca River Movement) of Colombia.[59] Here is an instance of an individual who is seized, equipped, and guided to reach out wondrously effectively to his own kind of people. This man, with his energy, insight, and vision, was a unique gift of the Holy Spirit to build His church. Murphy rightly concludes from this that the church must learn to recognize and trust Spirit-raised leadership.[60]

---

[55]Neill, *op. cit.,* pp. 318-319.

[56]Raymond J. Davis, *Fire on the Mountains. The Story of a Miracle — the Church in Ethiopia* (Grand Rapids, Michigan: Zondervan Publishing House, 1966). Cf. Peter Cotterall, "The Wave Theory of Church Propagation," *Church Growth Bulletin,* IX (May 1973).

[57] *Ibid.,* p. 7.

[58]Tippett, *Church Growth and the Word of God,* pp. 44-45.

[59] *God, Man and Church Growth,* pp. 328-340.

[60] *Ibid.,* pp. 339-340.

A close parallel to this is shown in Edgardo Silvoso's account of the Naranjo people movement in the area of San Nicolas, Argentina.[61] Pickett calls attention to the key persons in three of the movements which he has reviewed, namely, Vedamanickam, Venkayya, and Ditt.[62] McGavran remarks at one point:

> Basic to all these methods is a driving concern of some man or woman that others become disciples of the Lord Jesus Christ. This personal burden, like a stream in spate, makes a path for itself. The form of the path—the method—varies as in the previous illustrations according to the circumstances. But back of every method will be found a man who shares Christ's passion for the redemption of men.[63]

It must be stated that also in the Wallamo movement among the Galla peoples an indispensable role was played by such outstanding individuals as Wandaro, Dana Maja, Toro, and others. The personal element is always a factor in any movement.

Presently there is a large group movement taking place in the high Andes among the Indian peoples there. Among a population of some 10,000,000 peoples, thousands are turning to Christ by means of radio broadcasts and through zealous Christian witnessing on the part of new Christians. Dr. Abe Van Der Puy, President of HCJB, Quito, Ecuador, reports that in one province where just a few years ago the Christians numbered less than 500, at least 10,000 Christians are to be found there now.[64] Every day new groups of Christians in remote villages are being reported.

In several areas of Nigeria there are large groups of people who are moving to Christ. There is a continuing movement taking place among the Tiv people which appears to be a reaping on the basis of a cumulative effort of many years. It also appears to be the fruit of efforts put forth on a wide front. These efforts include early, difficult and unfruitful witnessing effort by some outstanding South African missionaries, early effort to reduce the language to writing and the production of the Bible in the Tiv language, widespread founding and functioning of elementary schools and classes for

---

[61]Edgardo Silvoso, "The Naranjo People Movement in Argentina," *Church Growth Bulletin*, XI (November 1974), 399-407.

[62]Pickett, *Christian Mass Movements in India*, p. 56.

[63]McGavran, *op. cit.*, p. 127.

[64]Talk given at breakfast at Holly's Landing, Grand Rapids, Michigan, Feb. 7, 1975, by Dr. Abe VanDerPuy on behalf of "The World Radio Missionary Fellowship, Inc." Cf. Henry Klaasen, "Remarkable Church Growth in High Ecuador," *Church Growth Bulletin*, IX (May 1973).

religious instruction, a parallel thirst on the part of the Tiv people for literacy, for education, and for reading materials; very effective use of a central hospital and of outlying dispensaries, very good rapport between the emerging Christian community and the large pagan Tiv community, the early emergence of some strong Tiv leadership in the church community, and the existence of a large homogeneous tribe of one and a half million Tiv people who are relatively independent and self-sufficient. Approximately 250,000 of the Tiv have been affected in a significant way by the impact of the gospel in their area.

To the east of the Tiv area among the foothills of the Cameroons on the border of Nigeria lies the Baissa district consisting of several small tribes of from 4500 to 7000 people apiece. They are the Kpanzo Jukun, Ichen, Chamba, Ndoro, and Tigum peoples with a smattering of Fulani, Tiv, Kuteb, and other tribes. In the period of 1950 to 1965, the Christian baptized community grew at a rate of 60% for that period. Of a population at that time of around 20,000 people, some 2000 had been profoundly influenced by the impact of the Christian faith. One of the key factors in the growth of the church in this area was the cosmopolitan character of the tribes who because of their smallness were forced to deal with, to live with, and even to marry people of other tribes. The striking thing about this area at that time was that nearly all of the young people between the ages of 14 and 23 were on the move. They were moving from animism either to Islam, Christianity, or to a form of secularism. At that moment in history the elders of the people who followed their traditional religion were worried lest they have no one to carry their pots of beer to their religious celebrations in the jungle. Hence, this particular period was a once-for-all period in the history of the Kasar Amana (Trust Territory) area. That was the time for harvesting among that peer group. The regrettable thing is that only a handful of old people were converted in the entire territory. This remains a cause for weakness in some sections of that church down to the present day. Most of the older people who came to Christ in that area were concentrated in one village. That particular village (approximately two-thirds of it) came with their chief en masse to Christianity. And in the early years the Christianity of that village was perhaps the strongest expression of Christianity in the area. At least it could immediately unfold, experiencing a sense of Christian community.

Finally, there is the question as to whether any of this history and process of group movements to Christ is transferable to the west, to the individualistic communities in Europe and North America.[65] It would appear that in one sense, there can be no repeating of the historical transitional period which has taken place in animistic socieites confronted by Christianity for the first time.[66] The west has gone through that period, and time can not be turned back. Secondly, I do not feel that it is very helpful to try to draw parallels with Soka Gakkai, the Value Creation Society of Japan, in its attracting power, nor with the peyote cult of the American Indians. It would appear to me that these instances are not clear cases of a transfer of ultimate loyalties.[67] However, this does not mean that we can continue to major on individualism and minor on the communal aspect of human nature. The weakness of the west in its sense of community may be calling the church to remember this aspect of man also in its gospel address of men of the west. Commerical advertising certainly has been built upon the homogeneous aspects of wide segments of the population in the west. The churches in the main have insisted on very individualistic professions of faith, and group seeking of baptism has been discouraged. We have sought to strip away all peer support from the convert; he is called upon to enter the body of Christ standing very much alone. This wide policy may stand in need of re-examination.

There is a widespread negative reaction to the attention the Church Growth school has directed to the Circle Church of Chicago and the hardhat church in Hammond, Indiana.[68] Both those who are seeking for the ecumenical character of the church and those who are seeking to fight the sin of racial prejudice raise many questions in this regard. The question which is invariably raised is: What *is* the church of Christ anyway? It is no doubt a problem which must be faced in this regard. Homogeneity is not an ultimate!

The Church Growth school has but recently moved into this area of seeking to apply Church Growth principles to the Eurican scene, and hence they must be given more time. All of us must wrestle with the character of so-called "post-Christian" U.S.A., England, France, etc. But we must

---

[65]Mc Gavran, *The Bridges of God,* p. 98.

[66]*Ibid.,* p. 112.

[67]Unless one wishes to equate peyote experience and the values of worldly success a la Soka Gakkai as idols claiming ultimate allegiance. Cf. Alan R. Tippett, "The Holy Spirit And Responsive Populations," in *Crucial Issues In Missions Tomorrow,* D. Mc Gavran ed. Chicago: Moody Press, 1972, pp. 82, 98.

[68]C. Peter Wagner, "American Church Growth: Update 1974," Paper: Fuller Seminary School of World Mission, p. 12.

beware of the debilitating effect of pessimism and defeatism, and we must pray that God will yet shake these nations and open new doors for the expansion of His kingdom. May God give us the eyes to see the open doors and obedient wills to enter such open doors as He may provide. In faith may we lay claim to the truth that even now the harvest is indeed "plenteous," but the laborers are few!

CHAPTER SIX

WHAT IS EVANGELISM?

by James I. Packer*

Evangelism and Theology

"Most evangelists," writes Michael Green, "are not very interested in theology: most theologians are not very interested in evangelism."[1]This testimony, alas, is true. Evangelism and theology for the most part go separate ways, and the result is great loss for both. When theology is not held on course by the demands of evangelistic communication, it grows abstract and speculative, wayward in method, theoretical in interest and irresponsible in stance. When evangelism is not fertilized, fed and controlled by theology, it becomes a stylized performance seeking its effect through manipulative skills rather than the power of vision and the force of truth. Both theology and evangelism are then, in one important sense, *unreal,* false to their own God-given nature; for all true theology has an evangelistic thrust, and all true evangelism is theology in action. That this double unreality exists today needs no proof from me. Seventy years ago, a generation after evangelism and theology had parted company in Scotland, James Denney pleaded for a reuniting of the two interests. "If evangelists were our theologians or theologians our evangelists, we should be nearer

*James I. Packer is Associate Principal of Trinity College, Bristol, England. A scholar of Corpus Christi College, Oxford, he was graduated in classical studies and philosophy in 1948 and in theology in 1950. He received his D. Phil. degree in 1954 for a thesis on the soteriology of Richard Baxter.

---

[1]Michael Green, *Evangelism in the Early Church* (London: Hodder and Stoughton, 1970), p. 7.

the ideal," he wrote; for "the evangelist is in the last resort the judge of theology. If it does not serve his purpose it is not true." For himself, he declared, "I haven't the faintest interest in any theology which doesn't help us to evangelize."[2] But Denney's words went unheeded, and the separation of theology and evangelism remains a characteristic fact of the late twentieth-century world.

It has been a fact of unhappy consequence for evangelism in several ways. First, it has led to evangelism being equated with revivalist procedures, or, at any rate, revivalism being regarded as evangelism *par excellence*. The revivalist pattern, with its special meetings and preachers, its aura of romance and excitement, its claims to supreme spiritual importance, and its methods and techniques for "drawing in the net" was created by such men as the "new school" Pelagian, Charles G. Finney,[3] and that much-loved exponent of the "simple gospel," Dwight L. Moody.[4] That God has worked, and worked wonderfully, through men who have used this pattern is undoubted, but one can still ask whether he has done so because of, or despite, this or that feature of it. Unfortunately, however, there is no agreed answer to such questions, for evangelical theology has done so little to evaluate the revivalist pattern in a theologically disciplined way. Pietistic and revivalist norms of "gospel preaching" and Christian conversion have tended either to be accepted uncritically or to be criticized undiscerningly. Revivalism has come under the hammer often enough from sacramentalist, liberal, radical and secularist standpoints, but these critiques, being shaped by doubts as to whether a definite conversion experience is valid or valuable, have not helped evangelicals who see this experience as biblical, beneficial and a privilege to assess what they say and do to induce it. Puffs for revivalism and squibs against it have come from evangelical sources, but little more; and meantime the updated revivalism of Dr. Billy Graham's crusades and organization continues as the greatest single force (so it would seem to the casual observer) in evangelism today.

Through revivalist crusades, and smaller ventures modelled on them,

---

[2]The quotations are from *The Death of Christ* (London: Hodder and Stoughton, 1902), p. vii; *The Expositor* (June 1901), p. 440; and James Moffatt's "Introduction" to *Letters of Principal James Denney to his Family and Friends* (London: Hodder and Stoughton, 1921), pp. xii f.; all cited by John Randolph Taylor, *God Loves Like That! The Theology of James Denney* (London: SCM Press, 1962), pp. 29 f.

[3]B. B. Warfield comments on Finney's Pelagian doctrine of plenary ability in *Perfectionism* (New York: Oxford University Press, 1931), II, pp. 173 ff.

[4]On Moody, cf. W. G. McLoughlin, *Modern Revivalism: Charles Grandison Finney to Billy Graham* (New York: The Ronald Press Company, 1959).

men and women are finding salvation, and for this one thanks God. Yet it cannot be denied that the situation as described has its problems. To his own embarrassment, the evangelist finds himself regarded as a nobler and wiser person than any theologian, and his methods viewed as a kind of sacred cow, which none may touch and against which none may speak. Also, those who evangelize by other than revivalist means (e.g., through the structures of Christian nurture in church and home) find themselves constantly under suspicion of neither understanding nor practicing evangelism at all. Also, such discussions of evangelism as arise under the shadow of revivalism regularly center upon the methods to employ rather than the message to convey; and this is most unhelpful, because it is in connection with the message that the deepest disagreements about evangelism emerge. For if you are (say) a universalist, construing the gospel as a call to wake up to the fact that we are all in a saved state; or a Tillichian, understanding "God" as the name for whatever is our "ultimate concern," or an old-style liberal, for whom the good news is that we are God's children by nature and can never be anything else; or one who thinks that to join the visible church is to enter the sphere of actual salvation automatically—then your evangelistic message, to which you invite response, will be significantly different from that of the man for whom the gospel is God's call to sinners to turn to Christ, for shelter from the wrath to come (cf. 1 Thess. 1:9 f.). To argue about methods while agreement on the message is lacking is inept; but revivalism, with its stress on techniques, has unfortunately encouraged this kind of ineptness.

The confusions indicated above have been augmented in recent years by the radical reconceiving of evangelism to which, as it seems, the World Council of Churches has now given its blessing.[5] Rejecting as paternalistic all idea of "propaganda" and "proselytizing"—that is, of making disciples and planting new churches—this novel concept identifies the church's evangelistic task as one of exhibiting the *shalom* (peace, harmony, human community, integrity and justice) which Jesus brought into the world, and of laboring to extend it where it is lacking. Evangelism thus ceases to be primarily a matter of speaking and becomes instead primarily a matter of practicing a serving presence among men. The true task of mission (it is said) is one of "entering into partnership with God in history to renew

---

[5]Cf., for evidence of this, *Eye of the Storm: The Great Debate in Mission,* ed. Donald McGavran (Waco: Word Books, 1972), and *The Evangelical Response to Bangkok,* ed. Ralph D. Winter (South Pasadena: William Carey Library, 1973).

society,"[6] and for this task the world must be allowed to write the agenda. In this context of a humanizing commitment, dialogue with men of other faiths and of no faith will certainly occur, but its aim will be to achieve mutual understanding and respect within the bonds of our common manhood rather than to persuade anyone to become a Christian. Thus evangelism is radically secularized. As C. Peter Wagner correctly puts it: "Whatever good works the church does, become evangelism, according to this definition. Harvey Cox says, for example, 'Any distinction between social action and evangelism is a mistaken one'.... Colin Williams agrees that 'the distinction between individual evangelism and evangelism calling for (social) changes is a false one'....This is 'presence evangelism.' A silent Christian presence, characterized by good works and charity, is called 'evangelism.' "[7] This is as far as possible from the revivalist idea of evangelism as the attempt to induce one-by-one personal conversion. One understands the desire of ecumenical missionary strategists to avoid giving any impression among the younger nations of ideological imperialism, and one applauds all who for Christ's sake seek to humanize a brutal and oppressive world; but one still has to ask, is there any correspondence between this essentially non-communicative program and *evangelism,* as the Bible presents it? If revivalist evangelism needs a little correction from Scripture, surely radical evangelism needs far, far more.

The Concept of Evangelism

If, now, we turn to the Bible and allow it to instruct us, we find that it yields a concept of evangelism that is Trinitarian and theocentric. Evangelism is usually defined as man's work, and this man-centeredness leads to many mistakes about it; but the basic biblical perspective is that evangelism is *a work of God.* God the creator, in the glory and power of his tri-unity, is both God the redeemer and God the evangelist. God's world lies under judgment because of mankind's apostasy and sin; "the wrath of God is revealed from heaven against all ungodliness and unrighteousness of men, who suppress the truth in unrighteousness" (Rom. 1:18). But God loves the world to which, because of sin, he is hostile; "God so loved the world, that he gave his only begotten Son, that whoever believes in him should not perish, but have eternal life" (John 3:16). He is the God who in

---

[6]J. G. Davies, *Dialogue with the World* (London: SCM Press, 1967), p. 15.
[7]C. Peter Wagner, *Frontiers in Missionary Strategy* (Chicago: Moody Press, 1971), p. 126.

love *sends*. The Father "loved us and sent his Son to be the propitiation for our sins" (I John 4:10); the Son brought us knowledge of the Father (John 14:9); now the Father and the Son have sent the Spirit to testify and give knowledge of the Son (John 14:26; 15:26; 16:14), and of his Father as our Father through him (cf. John 20:17). It is through the Spirit's agency that blind eyes and hard hearts are opened, so that Christ is acknowledged in his divine glory as our savior and Lord. "God, who said, 'Light shall shine out of darkness,' is the One who has shone in our hearts, to give the light of the knowledge of the glory of God in the face of Christ" (II Cor. 4:6). "No one can say, 'Jesus is Lord,' except by the Holy Spirit" (I Cor. 12:3)—but when the Spirit enlightens, this is precisely what men do say. Thus God in sovereign love overcomes the spiritual paralysis and perversity of the fallen human heart, and through this inward teaching by the Spirit draws us to himself (John 6:44 f., cf. I John 2:27). "If one may employ an anthropopathism and ascribe human feelings to God," wrote R. B. Kuiper—and surely he was right to think that one may—"God has a passion for souls,"[8] and this is how God expresses and satisfies it. He made us; he loved us; he ransoms us; he reclaims us. "Salvation is from the Lord" (Jonah 2:9).

But this is not the whole story. In the Bible evangelism is not only a work of God, it is also a work of man or rather *a work of God through man*. As God sent his Son to become man and so to "explain" him (cf. John 1:18), so now, adhering to the incarnational principle, if we may so speak, he sends Christian men to be heralds, ambassadors and teachers in His name and on His behalf. (These are the three main words that Paul uses to express his office as God's spokesman κῆρυξ, πρέσβυς, διδάσκαλος.) The task which God gives to his messengers is primarily and essentially one of proclamation, which the New Testament expresses chiefly by the use of three verbs with their cognate nouns: εὐαγγελίζομαι (tell the good news, εὐαγγέλιον); κηρύσσω (utter an announcement, κήρυγμα), and μαρτυρέω (bear witness, μαρτυρία). The proclamation is not, however, to be made on a casual, take-it-or-leave-it basis; the end in view is to "persuade" (πείθω, II Cor. 5:11 etc.), to "disciple" (μαθητεύω,

---

[8]R. B. Kuiper, *God-centered Evangelism: a Presentation of the Scriptural Theology of Evangelism* (Grand Rapids: Baker Book House, 1963), p. 95.

Acts 14:21), and so to "turn" or "convert" $\dot{\epsilon}\pi\iota\sigma\tau\rho\dot{\epsilon}\phi\omega$ verb which in this sense is used with the evangelist or the sinner, not God, as its subject, as when Paul tells Agrippa that Christ sent him to the Gentiles "to open their eyes so that they may turn (or, to turn them) from darkness to light" (Acts 26:18, cf. Luke 1:16; James 5:19f.). Evangelism, as I wrote elsewhere, is "communication with a view to conversion."[9]

Those who evangelize, then, are "working together" with God (II Cor. 6:1), and if they follow Paul's example they will never allow themselves to forget that all the power that comes through their witness, and all the fruit that results from it, is from God and not from themselves. I preached Christ crucified to you, wrote Paul to the Corinthians, in such a way that "your faith should not rest on the wisdom of men, but on the power of God....I planted, Apollos watered, but God was causing the growth" (I Cor. 2:5; 3:6, cf. Acts 19:9 f., where the "many people" in verse 10 are those Corinthians whom the Lord purposed to call to himself through Paul's preaching). Our gospel came to you, wrote Paul to the Thessalonians, "in power and in the Holy Spirit and with full conviction" (I Thess. 1:5); that explains why they received it "for what it really is, the word of God, which also performs its work in you who believe" (2:13). Paul sees their conviction as the fruit of their election, and so thanks God for their faith, which was his gift to them (1:2-5; 2:13). Luke shows the same perspective when he says of Lydia, "the Lord opened her heart to respond to the things spoken by Paul" (Acts 16:14).

Recognition that all the power and fruit of the word is from God and not from any human source does not, however, mean that the evangelist may disregard the human factors in persuasion. The ordinary principles of effective persuasion are not changed just because in a special way God is working through them. Paul was very conscious of the human factors in persuasion (cogency of statement, and empathetic concern), and he was most conscientious in observing them. He set no limit to what he would do to ensure that he did not, through personal insensitiveness or cultural inertia, set barriers and stumbling-blocks in the way of men's coming to Christ. "I have made myself a slave to all, that I might win the more. And to the Jews I became as a Jew, that I might win Jews...to those who are without law, as without law...that I might win those who are without law. To the weak I became weak, that I might win the weak; I have become all

---

[9] J. I. Packer, *Evangelism and the Sovereignty of God* (London: Inter-Varsity Fellowship, 1961), p. 85.

things to all men, that I may by all means save some" (I Cor. 9:19-22). It was to remove possible stumbling-blocks for Jews that Paul had Timothy circumcised (Acts 16:3) and also, it seems, Titus, though as he stressed he was under no compulsion to do this (Gal. 2:3). Paul's loving, imaginative adaptability in the service of truth and people is a shining example to all who engage in evangelism, and it cannot be pondered too often or taken too seriously.

But what in the last analysis determined Paul's view of his role as a "Christian persuader"[10] was his awareness that his ministry, like all Christian ministry, was both the form and the means of Christ's. It was Jesus Christ Himself, the risen Savior and enthroned Lord, who in and through Paul's evangelism "preached peace" (Eph. 2:17), and made his voice heard (Eph. 4:21; cf. John 10:16,27), and drew men to him (cf. John 12:32). The faith that sustained Paul in evangelism was that Christ would continue to do this, as in fact he had been doing everywhere that the gospel went (cf. Col. 1:6); and when Paul thought of his achievements in evangelism, his way of describing them was as *"what Christ has accomplished through me,* resulting in the obedience of the Gentiles by word and deed ... in the power of the Spirit"* (Rom. 15:18f.). To say that Paul, and all others who evangelize, work for the Lord is not untrue, but to speak of them as working together with him is truer, and to speak of him as as working through them is the most profound and precise truth of all.

There is one further way in which the concept of evangelism which we are building up needs extension, namely by reference to the message proclaimed. In the Bible, evangelism appears as *a work of God through men proclaiming Jesus Christ, and the new community in him.* Christian communication is not evangelism unless the full truth about Jesus is set forth. It is not enough to speak of the attractiveness of his person while omitting reference to the atoning significance of his work, as old-style liberals did. Nor is it enough to speak of his death as a sacrifice for sin if one declines to confess his deity, as Jehovah's Witnesses do. Nor will it suffice to dwell on his earthly life and impact while remaining agnostic about his physical resurrection, present reign, and approaching personal return, as is the common radical way. It is not adequate to point to Jesus' personal relationship with his disciples two millennia ago if we do not also declare that the glorified Jesus, though temporarily withdrawn from our sight,

---

[10]Title of a perceptive book by Leighton Ford on the work of a professional evangelist (New York: Harper and Row, 1966).

offers us just such a personal relationship today. For it is essentially this relationship that the Christian gospel is about. Jesus lives, and personal discipleship goes on. This, which from one standpoint is the central meaning of Jesus' resurrection and the outpouring of the Spirit, is from that same standpoint the evangelist's central message. And the new community belongs to this central message, for the call to become a disciple is also a call to become a partner with all other disciples. The question whether the church is part of the gospel used to be debated with some heat. If "church" is taken to mean a particular denomination or organization, viewed as an institute of salvation through its established channels of grace, the answer is certainly no. But if "church" means the brotherhood of God's children by adoption, into which all believers come and in the fellowship of which they find their God-intended fulness of life, then the answer must be yes. When John Wesley said that there is nothing so un-Christian as a solitary Christian, he spoke a profound truth. The gospel invites to fellowship, not merely with the Father and the Son, but with the saints too. What God calls us to is not "flight of the alone to the Alone," but life as a son in his worldwide family, where the rule is that our Father provides for each of us through the ministry of our brothers.

By the light of our concept of evangelism as a work of God we can now assess definitions of evangelism as a human activity. There is no reason why we should not define evangelism in this way, so long as subordination to God's purpose and dependence on God's power are duly stressed. Perhaps the best-known definition of this kind is that of the Archbishops' Committee on evangelism in the Church of England, which in 1918 stated that to evangelize is "so to present Christ Jesus in the power of the Holy Spirit, that men shall come to put their trust in God through Him, to accept Him as their Saviour, and serve Him as their King in the fellowship of His Church." In my book, *Evangelism and the Sovereignty of God,* I applauded this definition in all respects save its consecutive-clause wording, "that men *shall* come," which implies that the criterion of whether a particular activity is evangelism or not is whether or not it succeeds in converting anyone. The wording needed, I urged, was "that men *may* come," so that evangelism as an activity is unambiguously defined in terms of purpose rather than of consequence.[11] The resultant definition would then correspond exactly with the crisper formula of Michael Green: "Evangelism...is proclaiming the good news of salvation to men and

---

[11]Packer, *op. cit.,* pp. 37 ff.

women with a view to their conversion to Christ and incorporation in his church."[12] However, C. Peter Wagner takes me to task for making this proposal, in a rather muddled section of his otherwise stimulating book, *Frontiers in Missionary Strategy*. [13] The thesis Wagner wants to establish is that it is insufficient to conceive of evangelism as "presence" if this does not lead on to proclamation, and that proclamation in turn is insufficient if it does not issue in attempts at persuasion. This is certainly right. The need for positive attempts to persusade was one of the points which my own book most labored (see pp. 48-53, 75-82, 85, 92 f., 99 f., 103-106, 119-121). It is, therefore, disconcerting to find Wagner (who, incidentally, quotes Green's definition with warm approval) calling me "one who has considered the options and come out on the side of proclamation evangelism"—i. e., a view of evangelism which sees proclamation, not as a *means,* but as an *alternative* to persusasion.[14] I can assure Wagner (and my book is evidence) that that is an option I *never* considered!

Wagner seems to be pleading for two things. One is, uninhibited though non-manipulative attempts to persuade unbelievers to turn to Christ. He wants to see a vigorous pressing of "the well-meant gospel offer," the "free offer" of Christ, the invitation to "whosoever will" to take the water of life, the call to that exercise of faith which is at once the sinner's need and his duty. With this, in principle, I hope everyone will agree; certainly, as an admirer of Richard Baxter, Joseph Alleine, George Whitefield, Jonathan Edwards and C. H. Spurgeon, I do. The second thing Wagner advocates is the use of a pragmatic, short-term calculus of "success" in church-planting and church-growth as a guide to where it is, and is not, right to deploy

---

[12]Green, *op. cit.,* p. 7. My definition tallies also with that of the World Congress on Evangelism in Berlin, which is an expansion of that given by the Archbishops' Committee: "Evangelism is the proclamation of the Gospel of the crucified and risen Christ, the only Redeemer of men, according to the Scriptures, with the purpose of persuading condemned and lost sinners to put their trust in God by receiving and accepting Christ as Savior through the power of the Holy Spirit, and to serve Christ as Lord in every calling in life and in the fellowship of his church, looking towards the day of his coming in glory" (quoted from Wagner, *op.cit.,* p. 133).

[13] *Ibid.,* pp. 124-134.

[14]"Proclamation evangelism," Wagner explains, "measures success against the yardstick of how many people hear and understand the gospel message. This is often reported in terms of how many people are reached by attending a certain evangelistic campaign listening to a certain radio broadcast, or reading a certain piece of evangelistic literature" *(ibid.,* p. 132 ft.).

further missionary and evangelistic resources. This is much more disputable, but we cannot pursue discussion of it here.

Let me round off this section by quoting one further definition—Dr. George W. Peters' analysis of "evangelization" as "the authoritative presentation of the gospel of Jesus Christ as revealed in the Bible in relevant and intelligible terms, in a persuasive manner with the definite purpose of making Christian converts. It is a presentation-penetration-permeation-confrontation that not only elicits but demands a decision. It is preaching the gospel of Jesus Christ for a verdict."[15] Though there is no explicit reference here to the power and purpose of God or the church of Christ, the central emphasis on persuasion and conversion is in itself entirely right.

Educational Evangelism

One recurring problem when revivalist patterns of evangelism are followed, whether in single churches on in the "mass evangelism" of citywide campaigns, is that they allow so little room for instruction. From this it follows that where people are ignorant of biblical basics, these methods become inappropriate. Wisely did R. B. Kuiper say: "Historically the appeal of mass evangelism has been largely to the will and the emotions. That holds of the evangelistic preaching of both Wesley and Whitefield, to a limited extent to that of Jonathan Edwards, and most certainly to that of Dwight L. Moody, Charles G. Finney, Billy Sunday, and the Gypsy Smiths of more recent times. There was some justification for the nature of that appeal. All the aforenamed evangelists had good reason to assume on the part of their audiences a measure of knowledge of the basic teachings of Christianity. Today that assumption is no longer valid....The general populace is well-nigh abysmally ignorant of Bible history and Bible doctrine, as well as Bible ethics. In consequence, evangelistic preaching must today be first of all instructive."[16] Paul spoke of the "the gospel, for which I was appointed a preacher ... *and a teacher"* (II Tim. 1:10 f.), and said of Christ, "we proclaim him ... *teaching every man* with all wisdom" (Col. 1:28). In both texts the reference to teaching is explanatory of the reference to preaching; Paul saw himself as a teaching preacher, an educational evangelist, and it is vitally important at the present time that we should confine ourselves to patterns of evangelistic practice which allow

---

[15]George W. Peters, *A Biblical Theology of Missions* (Chicago: Moody Press, 1972), p. 11.
[16]Kuiper, *op.cit.*, p. 163.

for thorough instruction, after Paul's example. For there is in fact a good deal to be conveyed.

If we ask, What is the evangelistic message?, the New Testament seems to show that there are essentially five points on which instruction must be given.

First, the gospel is a message about *God;* telling us that He is our maker, in whom we exist and move each moment and in whose hands, for good or ill, we always are, and that we, his creatures, were made to worship and serve Him and to live for His glory. These are the foundation-truths of theism, and upon them the gospel is built. The Jews of New Testament days, with Old Testament faith behind them, knew these things, and when the apostles preached to Jews they could take them for granted. But when Paul preached to Gentiles, whose background was polytheistic, it was with theism that he had to start. So, when the Athenians asked him to explain his talk about Jesus and the resurrection, he began by telling them about God the creator. "God...made the world...he himself gives to all life and breath and all things...and he made...every nation...that they should seek God" (Acts 17:24-27). This was not, as is sometimes supposed, a piece of philosophical apologetic which Paul afterwards regretted, but the first and basic lesson in theistic faith. Modern men are for the most part as ignorant about creation and creaturehood as were the ancient Athenians; like Paul, therefore, we must start in evangelizing them by telling them of the Creator whom they have forgotten to remember, and go on from there.

Second, the gospel is a message about *sin.* It defines sin as failure to meet the holy Creator's total claim, and it diagnoses sin in us, telling us that we are helpless slaves of our own rebelliousness, showing ourselves under the righteous judgment of God, and assuring us that nothing we do for ourselves can put us right. Not till we have begun to grasp these things can we see what it means to say that Jesus Christ saves from sin. All sorts of awarenesses of need are symptoms of sin; much of the task of evangelistic instruction is to take occasion from these symptoms to diagnose the real disease, and thus bring to light "the problem behind the problem," our fundamental wrongness with God.

Third, the gospel is a message about *the person and work of Christ;* an interpreted story of the earthly life, death, resurrection and reign of God's Son. Both the facts and the meaning must be given. Whether or not we use the technical terms, "incarnation," "atonement" and so forth, we must teach what they express—who Jesus was, in relation both to the Father and to us, and what He did as His Father's will for us. It is sometimes said that it is the presentation of Christ's person, rather than of doctrines about Him, that draws sinners to His feet, and it is certainly true that it is the living Christ who saves, and that a theory of atonement, however orthodox, is no substitute for a savior. But Jesus of Nazareth cannot be known as the living Christ if we are unaware that He was eternal God and that His passion, His judicial murder, was really His redeeming action of bearing away men's sins. We cannot see Jesus as a personal savior till we see this, nor can we know how to approach Him till we have learned that the man of Galilee now reigns as God's king, and must be hailed as such.

Fourth, the gospel is a message about *new birth,* telling us that our plight in sin is so great that nothing less than a supernatural renewing of us can save us. There has to be a wholly new beginning, through the power of the Holy Spirit.

Fifth, the gospel summons us to *faith, repentance and discipleship*. Faith is not a mere feeling of confidence, nor repentance and discipleship. Faith is not a mere feeling of confidence, nor repentance a mere feeling of remorse; both are dynamic states of the whole man. Faith is credence and conviction regarding the gospel message, and it is more; born of self-despair, it is essentially a casting and resting of oneself on the promises of Christ and the Christ of those promises. Repentance is a changed attitude of heart and mind, leading to a new life of denying self and serving the Saviour as king in self's place. And discipleship is a matter of relating oneself to the living, exalted Christ as a learner and a follower, and to the rest of Christ's disciples as one who longs both to learn from them and to give to them, and who knows that his master's will is for him to be in their company.

This, in outline, is the evangelistic message, and it needs to be thoroughly taught everywhere where it is not already thoroughly known. It is the Holy Spirit's work to make sinners repent and believe, but it is our task and responsibility to make sure that they are clear what the gospel is, how it affects them, and why and how they should respond to it; and until we are sure that a person has graspsed these things, we are hardly in a position to press him to commit himself to Christ, for it is not yet clear that he is in a position really and responsibly to do so. Whatever means and structures we use in evangelism, all the points listed must be taught. If we tried to short-circuit the process of instruction and to precipitate "decisions" without it, we should merely produce psychological upsets; people would come to our vestries and counselling sessions in an agitated state; they would go through motions of commitment at our bidding, but when the shock wore off it would appear that their decision meant nothing save that now they are to a greater or less extent "gospel-hardened." And if a few proved to be truly converted, that would be despite our methods rather than because of them.

It is no part of my present task to attempt judgments on any particular ways of evangelism that are practiced today, but it is surely plain from what has been said that there can be no safer or more natural milieu for evangelism than the steady teaching, witnessing and nurturing of the local church.

Response to the Gospel

This essay is seeking to spell out a normative theological concept of evangelism, by which any attempted reformation of evangelism in our day will need to be controlled. One further matter requires discussion for the clarifying of this concept, namely the nature of the response which evangelism requires. So far, we have spoken of it as conversion, involving faith, repentance and discipleship; but this formula is not clear enough in its meaning, and we must take the analysis further.

The common pietistic and revivalist understanding, present at presuppositional level even when it is not made theologically explicit, is that the gospel of God is meant to induce a characteristic *conversion-experience*. This is conceived as a compound of two elements: the experience of receiving, and committing oneself to, the God and the Christ of the gospel, and the experience of receiving assurance from that God, so that one knows oneself pardoned and accepted by him. The relative emphasis on these two elements has varied: in the eighteenth century, for example, the stress was on assurance ("finding peace"), in the twentieth it has been on commitment ("decision for Christ"); but it is constantly assumed that where there is one there will also be the other. In the pietistic-revivalist tradition, evangelistic procedures (meetings, sermons, tracts, conversational techniques) have all been shaped by the desire that God should use them to induce conversion-experiences, and the belief that this is precisely what He wills to do. But here some comments must be made.

First, it must be said that while a conversion-experience, like any other particular conscious encounter with a gracious God, is a precious gift, and while no adult can turn to God and live to God without some experiences of this encounter (the Holy Spirit will see to that), the Bible teaches no doctrine of God-given experiences as such. It defines God's purpose and work in men's lives in terms, not of experiences, but of relationships, and though relationships issue in experiences, the two things are not the same. God's work in our lives, whereby He creates and deepens our love-relationship with Himself, is more than experience (for it is an actual transformation of our being, in ways which do not yet fully appear), and it is beyond experience (for the experiences which are its product are far less than its measure; much of what God does in us is not directly experienced). To say, then, what is true—that God wills through our evangelism to work in unbelievers and call them effectually to himself—is something bigger than, and somewhat different from, saying that God will through our evangelism induce conversion-experiences.

Second, it must be said that this particular concept of a conversion-experience, while its ingredients are biblical in themselves, is a construct from these ingredients in the light of much Protestant Christian experience since the Reformation, rather than being a biblical norm.

Third, it must be said that what the Bible looks for in Christians is not the consciousness of a conversion-experience, but the evidence of a converted state; and its angle of interest when dealing with actual conversions is motivational rather than psychological—that is, its purpose is not to tell us what men who turned to God felt like, so that we can imaginatively put ourselves in their shoes, but to show us how God actually met them and moved them to go his way. The signs of convertedness are simply the marks of discipleship, the marks, that is, of being one of the Lord's *learners*—namely, a structured knowledge of God in Christ, which the learner seeks constantly to deepen and augment; a practical recognition of total and controlling commitment to God and His will, and to Christ and His people; and an awareness that knowing and enjoying God is man's true life (just as it is his chief end), which leads him to press on resolutely to know his Lord better, at any cost and by any road, and to look ahead with eagerness to the glory that is promised when Jesus comes again.

Fourth, it must be said that the more we concentrate on inducing, isolating and identifying conversion-experiences, the more risk we run of misunderstanding and misrepresenting the course of actual experience. For it is not always possible to isolate the moment of conversion. God leads some into a firm faith-relationship with himself by a series of imperceptible steps, so that the precise moment of passage from death to life cannot be picked out for inspection. (This is the case in many Bible biographies.) Conversely, it is only too possible to induce in the susceptible experiences of supposed conversion which do not develop into discipleship or a meaningful church commitment, but issue in nothing—as happened in the Cornish revivals of the last century, in which folk "got converted" time and again without any real change of heart; and as seems to have happened during the first decade of Evangelism in Depth in Latin America.[17]

What this means is that in all evangelism our aim must be nothing less than to make men Christ's disciples in the community of disciples; that we must constantly check our evangelistic structures to ensure that this aim comes through clearly; and that we leave people in no doubt that the response we hope to see in them is convertedness rather than a particular conversion-experience. Also, the question arises whether, instead of isolating individuals in order to pursue with them the issues of personal commitment, which is a basic revivalist technique, we should not give priority to evangelizing them in their natural human groupings—in the West, for instance, the nuclear family; in other countries, the extended family (the clan), or the tribe—seeking a discipleship - commitment from the group, and from individuals as members of it. This would be a step back towards the evangelistic style of the apostolic age, which, as Harry R. Boer notes, was marked by "the conversion of *families* or *households*. The Church was not built up of so many individual Christians but of *basic social units,* of *organic wholes,* and these units, these wholes, were the fundamental cells of society, namely *families.* [18] Is this part of what the reformation of evangelism in our day might mean?

The view of evangelism put forward in this essay is conceived in terms of God and His message primarily, and of man and his methods only secondarily. It affirms that what man says and does in evangelism must be determined by what God is doing, and that the divine message itself must determine the aims and methods of the human messengers. To discuss in detail how this approach might bear on contemporary evangelistic practice is beyond my scope—and, I think, my competence. I limit myself to offering an overall concept of evangelism, crystallized from Scripture as best I can; and I hope it may make some small contribution towards the reform and renewal of evangelism which, on any showing, is a major need at this time.

---

[17]Cf. Wagner, *op.cit.,* pp. 139-160.

[18]Harry R. Boer, *Pentecost and Missions* (London: Lutterworth Press, 1961), p. 165.

CHAPTER SEVEN

CHURCH-MISSION RELATIONSHIPS

by Harvie M. Conn.

The Tension Points

This chapter will focus on the relationships between the national church and the "foreign" mission in the area to which that church is, in some way, related. Opening up this question of church/mission tensions today is like opening up Pandora's can of worms.

The most recent full-scale study of the topic within evangelical circles at Green Lake, Wisconsin, 1971, by leaders of the Evangelical Foreign Missions Association and the Interdenominational Foreign Missions Association illustrates the difficulties involved.[1]

As Dr. Ralph Winter noted, the Conference intended to focus on "the relations between an American *mission* and an overseas national *church* ....To these mission/church relations, GL '71 added church/mission relations, namely the relation of the *churches* back home to the *mission* they support."[2] And since GL '71, the triad of church/mission/church relationship has expanded, with our awareness of missions from the third world, into the further complications of church/mission/church/mission-/church. The end is not in sight.[3]

For several reasons, GL '71 must be deemed a frustrating experience.

---

[1]See the volume edited by Vergil Gerber, *Missions in Creative Tension* (South Pasadena, Ca.: William Carey Library, 1971), where the preparatory and discussion papers were gathered. It is disappointing that the Lausanne Covenant, apart from some very general remarks, did not speak out on this question in any formed way (J. D. Douglas, editor, *Let the Earth Hear His Voice* Minneapolis: World Wide Publications, 1975, pp. 5-6).

[2]Peter Wagner, editor, *Church/Mission Tensions Today* (Chicago: Moody Press, 1972), p. 133.

[3]The expansion into what Winter calls "third generation church planting," however, does not seem to us to go too far beyond the original one of the relationship between the national church and the foreign mission which has established or encouraged it.

One of the objectives of the Conference was "to identify the points of tension which exist today between mission and church."[4] That objective was not adequately reached. A token number of nationals played less than even consultative roles in that analysis. Sixteen tension areas were isolated, and of these, fifteen were basically oriented to person-to-person relationships in administrative procedures. Administrative problems were probably given the largest bulk of time.[5] Without prejudging the importance of either personal or administrative tensions, we would only comment that even these areas involve theological dimensions which were left unexplored. The only radical theological perspectives were provided by Edmund P. Clowney's morning messages on "The Biblical Doctrine of the Ministry of the Church (Biblical Ecclesiology and the Crisis in Missions)."[6] And, judging from the essays published after Green Lake, they played little normative part in the structuring of solutions.[7] The activism of American evangelical missions thinking continued to present the picture of a "church without theology" and a "mission without theology." Biblical theology functioned on a devotional, not a canonical level.

The third objective of Green Lake, "to develop guidelines which will help each mission to chart its own individual course of action...," also found minimal resolution. The Affirmation passed unanimously at the end of the Conference confessed "failure in building scriptural bridges of unity and fellowship between North America and overseas churches." It urged mission societies "to discover forms of church-mission-church relationships that allow for the fullest scriptural expression of the missionary nature and purpose of the church."[8]

These gaps between objectives and achievements may come from a deeper failure to really explore scriptural principles in a formative way. Neither personal nor administrative questions were examined from this theological perspective. And beyond them, lying untouched and presumed, were the structural questions of the legitimacy of foreign mission over against national church.[9]

---

[4]Gerber, *op. cit.,* p. 113.

[5]*Ibid.,* pp. 347-350.

[6]*Ibid.,* pp. 231ff.

[7]Wagner, *op. cit.* The only essay that shows a real attempt to grapple with this material in a radical way is that by Dr. Jack F. Shepherd, "Is the Church Really Necessary?."

[8]Gerber, *op. cit.,* p. 383.

[9]So, the recorder of the discussion group on "Theological Differences" notes, as a main feature of his presentation, "points of tension over theological differences between missions and the receiving churches, largely over the question as to which agency is given biblical authority to make decisions in overlapping areas such as outreach and evangelism" *(ibid.,* p. 368).

We are convinced that, as long as evangelical missions theory continues to develop on a purely functional level, without the operative judgment of biblical theology, the tension areas cannot be isolated and solutions cannot be found.[10] We are also convinced that the tension areas of a basic sort are theological in nature. They are:

1. What is the biblical justification for the existence of the foreign mission apart from the national church? Are the categories of modalities and sodalities normative tools in understanding the relationship of church and mission?[11]

2. What is missions? Is its focus "on the world, not on the church."[12] On "evangelism," in isolation from service (the Church Growth school)?

3. What relationship should the missionary sustain to his national brothers? How should his gifts be exercised and disciplined in that part of the body of Christ where he is called to serve?[13]

Theoretical Approaches to the Problem

Evangelical formulations through the nineteenth century revolved around the justification of free missionary societies outside and beside the church. Nineteenth century missiology adopted what Gerhard Hoffmann has called a "phenomenological approach" to the problem.[14] The

---

[10]Orlando Costas comes close to saying this when he writes, "Viewed from the perspective of biblical theology, the church-mission issue is imbedded in several crucial theological questions...."*(The Church and Its Mission: A Shattering Critique From the Third World* Wheaton: Tyndale House, 1974 p. 160). However,he also sees the tension as historical (the ambiguous origin of the modern missionary movement), sociopolitical (the context of the contemporary missionary enterprise), strategic (a church that is not indigenous as the agent of evangelism), cultural (the mission as an agent for the promotion of the gospel and its own national culture). These factors, we contend, complicate the basic problem, but they are not part of the core tension. They are important but not foundational.

[11]This is the language developed particularly by Ralph Winter in *The Warp and the Woof* (South Pasadena, Ca.: William Carey Library, 1971), pp. 52-62, to achieve clarification over church-mission relationships. Cf. also C. Peter Wagner, *Frontiers in Missionary Strategy* (Chicago: Moody Press, 1971), pp. 177-178.

[12]Gerber, *op. cit.,* p. 208.

[13]This third question is an attempt to give theological focus and prominence to the problems of person-to-person relationships emphasized at Green Lake.

[14]Gerhard Hoffmann, "Considerations on Integration of Church and Mission in Germany," *International Review of Mission,* Vol. 58 (July, 1969), 278ff.

missionary movement was not "fundamentally interested in theological problems" as much as urgency in action. And any theological study presupposed either consciously or unconsciously a theological justification of missionary agencies as separate bodies outside the established churches. The separate structures of church and mission was "a fact that needed theological justification rather than serious questioning."[15] A contemporary pattern had begun to emerge."Thus, the rediscovery of mission in the nineteenth century did not challenge the structures of the established churches" or the structures of establishing missions. It left "most of the mission societies...quite content to be tolerated by the established churches as separate spiritual societies."[16]

Against this background, the first theorizing began to be formulated. James Scherer lists three factors that prompted this early study. (1) The problem of continuity and growth on the fields pressed for some development of national church structure. (2) Mission societies were also becoming concerned about the proper use of their limited funds and personnel. "Too many missionaries were tied up in a given area for too long under paternalism."[17] (3) A better understanding between mission societies and churches in the homeland was developing. Up till now, missions had been largely the work of independent societies. Now, due in part to the Evangelical Awakening, churches began to take a more friendly attitude toward missions. Pietistic patterns formed by individualism and voluntarism began to give way to church-centered missionary methods. This was particularly so in missions-sending groups from the United States.[18]

Out of this discussion, and particularly from the pens of Henry Venn and Rufus Anderson, came "the indigenous church concept." R. Pierce Beaver, speaking of that concept, has noted that "there was no rival theory of missions set forth in North America during the nineteenth and first half of

---

[15] *Ibid.*, 279.

[16] *Ibid.*, 280.

[17] James Scherer, *Missionary Go Home!* (Englewood Cliffs, N.J.: Prentice-Hall, 1964), p.90. Within the Church Missionary Society, for example, a severe financial crisis in 1841 helped to create the atmosphere for reviewing Society policy. Henry Venn began his work as Secretary in that very year.

[18] In the Church Missionary Society, for example, Venn worked out an arrangement tying the independent society much more closely to the Church of England. A new clause in the Constitution enabled the church's bishops to see the Society "as a voluntary organization cooperating with them in their work." The change implied that the Society was the handmaid of the church and that there might come further changes in the future. Peter Beyerhaus and Peter Lefever, *The Responsible Church and the Foreign Mission* (Grand Rapids: Eerdmans Publ. Comp., 1964), p. 26.

the twentieth century....The indigenous church theory of Roland Allen is hardly more than a later restatement of the Anderson-Venn system."[19]

Best known for its "three-self formula," the heart of the concept, as Henry Venn developed it, was commitment to the establishment of "a genuinely native church."[20] He saw the aim of missions as "the establishment of a Native Church under Native Pastors upon a self supporting system" and the Mission's "euthanasia" when that aim was achieved.[21] Through three stages of gradual relaxation of control, the missionary was to superintend the emergence of a forming church from "Christian companies" to national churches administered and subsidized by the mission to a native episcopate. The final relinquishment of foreign authority over the established church and the transfer of the mission's attention to new unevangelized fields was the final step, the euthanasia of the mission.

Venn's insights were revolutionary in his day. The threefold formulation was meant to guarantee the native church its proper dignity as a people of God. "After a long period of patriarchal, individualistic missionary work, he pointed the way to a 'church-centric' mission...."[22] His analysis set up the limits of the problem even today.

At the same time, it also set up the weaknesses of the solution. (1) In effect, he made self-support the sole criterion of the selfhood of the church. Even today, it has the effect of ignoring the Reformation marks of the church in defining a missionary church, and this amplifies the cleavage between the so-called "sending church" and the "receiving church." (2) It creates a definition of the missionary severely restricting him to the role of pioneer church planter, an evangelist. The missionary's responsibility to the local church ceases as the church reaches towards integrity. This definition, with modifications, continues to be strongly supported by the writing of such men as Donald McGavran and Peter Wagner.[23] (3) Such formulations do not altogether escape the charges of the paternalism and colonialistic control. Even past the first stage of church planting, the pastor remains responsible to the missionary, rather than to all the body of Christ and its Lord. And always the practice of subsidy ties the national to the

---

[19]*Christusprediking in de Wereld* (Kampen: J. H. Kok, 1965), p. 61.

[20]Max Warren, editor, *To Apply the Gospel: Selections From the Writings of Henry Venn* (Grand Rapids: Eerdmans Publ. Comp., 1971), p. 25.

[21]*Ibid.,* p. 28.

[22]Beyerhaus and Lefever, *op. cit.,* p. 30.

[23]Donald McGavran, editor, *Crucial Issues in Missions Tomorrow* (Chicago: Moody Press, 1972), pp. 9-12; Wagner, *op. cit.,* pp. 215ff.

missionary. (4) Because of this learning relationship and the identification of the missionary's role with pioneer evangelism, the "church development syndrome"[24] the stagnation of the national church's own evangelistic program, will always be a real danger.[25]

Discussions within the International Missionary Council have tended increasingly to focus on the weaknesses of both the terminology and the structural relation of church and mission implicit in the evangelical tradition surrounding the indigenous concept. Tacit discontent seems first to have surfaced at the Jerusalem 1928 Conference as the number of delegates from so-called younger churches increased (one fifth of those attending). Stephen Neill saw the new mood in the 1925 remarks of Dr. S. C. Leung, leader of the Church of Christ in China:

> It seems to me that the time has come when the missions and missionaries might well consider the question of reorganizing themselves on a different basis, so that the missions and the Chinese Church will hereafter not appear as two parallel organizations, and that all activities initiated, maintained and financed by the missions should be expressed only through the Chinese Church. This means the recognition of the Chinese Church as the chief centre of responsibility, the transfer of the responsibility now attached to the missions to the Chinese Church, the willingness of the missions to function only through the Chinese Church, and the willingness of the individual missionaries to function as officers of the Church, and no longer as mere representatives of the mission boards, who are entirely beyond the control of the Chinese Church...."[26]

Especially in the Conferences that followed World War II, the withdrawal of missionaries from leadership roles in the overseas church was formulated into a more explicitly theoretical structure. The theme of

---

[24]C. Peter Wagner uses this language repeatedly in speaking of the church's temptation to limit its ministry to church development, "the *inward* ministry of the Church, all that is involved in perfecting believers and making them better servants of Christ" (*Symposium of the Papers Presented at the Annual Meeting of the Association of Evangelical Professors of Missions,* December, 1972, p. 34; Wagner, *op. cit.,* p. 231).

[25]Beyerhaus notes, in this connection, that there were several decades of such retarded growth in India subsequent to Venn's reforms (*op. cit.,* p. 29). Such was not Venn's own purpose (Warren, *op. cit.,* p. 63). But his built-in structure may have led to this result.

[26]Stephen Neill, *History of Christian Missions* (Grand Rapids: Eerdmans Publ. Comp., 1964), pp. 516-517.

the Whitby 1947 Assembly was "partners in obedience," and behind the theme was increasing western recognition of "full spiritual equality" in a "common calling."

In the years between Whitby and Willingen 1952, increasingly it was discovered "that the slogan and the perspective were inadequate. The partnership in mission is not only in the lands of the younger church. It is on a global front, in every nation."[27] The focus of the Whitby theme was said to increase the isolation of church from mission, rather than reduce it. "It gave the young church the chance to restrict, and even to obstruct, the obedient 'older Church' in following its own call to Mission."[28] This was done by the growing insistence on the part of the younger church that future missionaries should come as fraternal workers and obey the instructions of indigenous church leaders.[29]

At Willingen, the theme of *The World Mission of the Church* shifted further the accent from Missions to Mission. Lines of witness were to run through every nation to all frontiers where Jesus Christ was not recognized as Lord and in mission, the distinctions between older and younger churches were to be removed.

At Willingen, the Anderson-Venn formula came under open attack in the report of Commission II.

> The accepted definition of an independent church, which has all too often been confused with a definition of an indigenous church, as 'self-supporting, self-governing and self-propagating' community needs to be reconsidered....If self-sufficiency and autonomy are isolated as ends in themselves they lead to a dangerous narrowness of view. They have meaning only as expressions of the church's worshipping and witnessing character. We need to apply tests deeper in content and wider in scope. These should follow from the church's nature as a worshipping, witnessing and expectant body.[30]

The Willingen report then went on to describe these deeper tests of indigeneity. Since the indigenous church is only "the universal church in its local setting," indigenization should find expression first of all in the

---

[27]R. Pierce Beaver, *From Missions to Mission* (New York: Association Press, 1964), pp. 78-79.

[28]Beyerhaus and Lefever, *op. cit.,* p. 168.

[29]Peter Beyerhaus, "The Three Selves Formula: Is it Built on Biblical Foundations?" *International Review of Missions,* Vol. 53 (October, 1964), p. 397.

[30]Norman Goodall, ed., *Missions Under the Cross* (London: Edinburgh House Press, 1953), pp. 195-196.

church's witness and worship. Four marks of such a church in its indigeneity were stressed: (1) Relatedness to the soil, ability to make elements of local cultures captive to Christ (2) Possession of an adequately trained ministry, a ministry adapted to local requirements (3) An inner spiritual life, nurturing the Christian community, witnessing to the unevangelized (4) Membership in the church universal. This was to find expression in the concept of partnership in obedience and mutual help toward other churches.

Since Willingen, ecumenical discussions have focused on other issues. But those earlier debates have indicated a deeper sensitivity to the problem than the Johnny-come-lately formulations of the 1966 Wheaton Congress and Green Lake 1971. The growing consensus of the ecumenical formulations has pointed to an earlier willingness on the part of conciliar-related churches and missions to attempt more radical changes in given structures and methodologies than evangelicals outside the circle have been willing to try.

At the same time, the ecumenical discussions have left unresolved problems. Herbert Jackson, former director of the Missionary Research Library, saw in the subservience of mission to younger church the rise of an unintentional "tyranny...which stifles apostolate and militates very greatly against any real fulfillment of the great commission and against the freedom of the Holy Spirit to move where He will...."[31] From this has come what Jackson feels to be "a retraction in the missionary witness that is worse than tragic." The problems that arose after Whitby seem to remain with us.

The Church Growth school has responded to this impasse by underlining and refining earlier evangelical theory. Structural changes are regarded as secondary in importance "if principles governing cordial relationships are stated regardless as to whether they guarantee an ever more effective evangelization...Church-Mission relationships have little importance in themselves. They are important chiefly if they enable effective discipling of men and ethne to take place."[32] For Donald McGavran, the crucial question is not a structural one, but a teleological one. Have missionary

---

[31] Herbert C. Jackson, "Some Old Patterns For New in Missions," *Occasional Bulletin of the Missionary Research Library*, Vol. 12, No. 10 (December, 1961), p. 5. Quoted in: McGavran, *op. cit.*, p. 116; and *Church/Mission Tensions Today*, pp. 48-49.

societies lost their identity as *missionary* societies? *"In every genuine missionary agency, evangelism should continue 'a chief and irreplaceable part' of the total action,"*[33]McGavran's insistence is not for "missionary societies to do evangelism and nothing else. The call, rather, is to make sure that, in the plethora of desirable good deeds, evangelism is *not crowded out."*[34]

It is this same perspective that colors the fears of C. Peter Wagner for what he calls the "syndrome of church development" and "the Babylonian captivity of the Christian mission." Warning against even the establishment of "the indigenous church" as a proper goal of the Christian mission if the end result is the creation of a church "completely free of foreign ties, and yet...an exotic enclave with little relevance to the wider cultural context,"[35] he properly speaks of "indigenization becoming merely a mask for irresponsibility. Indigenous principles, after all, are only a means, not an end in themselves."[36] The missionary who sets the perfecting of the emerging church as his *ultimate* goal "may not only lose hold of his first love (that of reaching the lost), but he also runs the serious risk of *harming* the church with an overdose of paternalism."[37] Churches planted and nurtured by the mission must themselves launch missions and missionary work. The pattern must move "from mission to church to mission."[38]

Along with this strong insistence on the evangelistic goals of church and

---

[33]Donald McGavran, Will Green Lake Betray the Two Billion?" *Church Growth Bulletin*, Vol. 7, No. 6 (July, 1971), 152.

[33]McGavran, *Crucial Issues in Missions Tomorrow*, p. 199. The italics are those of the author.

[34]*Ibid.* It is however problematic to me whether this is McGavran's consistent emphasis. Earlier, in the introduction to this same volume, McGavran distinguishes sharply between what he calls the scope of the task of "Biblical missions or missionary missions" and the scope of the church's ministry. "The duty of the church," he writes, "is, of course, much wider than missionary missions....The Church, but not the mission, touches all of life. The mission has its specific sphere of activity — the communication of the gospel. The missionary society is not the church, even as the surgeon is not the hospital" (p. 10). And again, "It is essential to see the distinction between the church doing such things on budgets and with organizations created for social action of this sort — which is good — and the missionary society doing them — which is bad. The missionary society was created for the specific task of discipling the nation" (p. 12).

[35]Wagner, *Frontiers in Missionary Strategy*, p. 162.

[36]*Ibid.*, p. 169.

[37]*Ibid.*, p. 170. The merger of the International Missionary Council with the World Council of Churches is regarded as "undoubtedly the most notorious example of this in modern times *(Symposium of the Papers Presented*, p. 43). "Because of the legitimate feeling that Third World men had to be present in the IMC, someone along the way started inviting *churchmen* to a *missionary* organization...The Babylonian captivity had begun..." (p. 44).

[38]Wagner, *Frontiers in Missionary Strategy*, p. 176.

mission, the school has not neglected the questions of structure. Ralph Winter has given special attention to this question in his argument for the necessity not only of "modalities" (vertically-structured groupings which have no age or sex limitations, such as churches) but of "sodalities" (horizontal or ecclesiastical and para-ecclesiastical structures engaged in interdenominational, nonecclesiastical mission in the field).[39] Arguing from the goal-oriented perspective that characterizes the Church Growth school, Winter sees sodalities as historically a large factor in the expansion of the church, exemplified in the Catholic orders and Protestant voluntary societies.[40] He sees the tension areas between church and mission as a tension between modalities and sodalities, and the resolution of much of these tensions in the realization that "churches need missions, because modalities need sodalities."[41] Modalities he judges to be "characteristically impotent apart from careful maintenance of consensus, whether they are civil or ecclesiastical structures."[42] They must acknowledge and foster the mobility and striking power of mission sodalities. Even the national church modality needs to be sprinkled with such sodalities for good church health.

The concern of the school for the "church development syndrome" is a legitimate one. The historical case for a neglect of evangelism by national church and foreign mission cannot be put aside easily. But "the compulsion to dissolve the mission and become church" need not necessarily "be seen as a symptom of the syndrome...."[43] It may rather flow from the conviction that "there is no ground in the New Testament for a concept of mission apart from the church, just as there is no concept of the church apart from mission."[44] "The biblical-theological model of the church does not allow for a missionary structure apart from the church. Sodalities ought to function structurally apart from modalities only when the church loses sight of her missionary responsibility and fails to acknowledge the diverse gifts which the Spirit bestows upon her to fulfill the multiple dimensions of the missionary mandate."[45]

The failure of the Church Growth school's analysis of church-mission structures is not a failure to see "that structures in themselves become

---

[39]Winter, *op. cit.*, pp. 52ff.

[40] *Ibid.*, p. 57.

[41] *Ibid.*, p. 62.

[42] *Ibid.*, p. 60.

[43]Contra. Wagner, *Symposium of the Papers Presented*, p. 419

[44]Costas, *op. cit.*, p. 168.

[45] *Ibid.*, p. 169.

sources of tension."[46] Winter's discussion focuses on that very tension. Nor is it a failure to acknowledge that "...wrong structures do restrict dynamic."[47] Given a more biblical-theological framework for the understanding of structure, that insight is important. The basic problem lies in Wagner's insistence that such structural questions are secondary since "the New Testament gives us no inspired structure for mission/church relationships. Fusion, modified fusion, dichotomy, modified dichotomy, unilaterally, functional partnership, parallelism — all are options with more or less validity according to the circumstances and according to the degree they help or hinder the fulfillment of the Great Commission."[48] The basic problem is in choosing "the structure of mission-church relationship on pragmatic grounds,"[49] conceiving of the church sociologically and then seeking for nominal scriptural warrant for an institution that has already been defined. In the language of Edmund Clowney, "we cannot restrict the authority of Christ to the *content* of the gospel by which his people are saved while claiming for ourselves the right to decide upon the *form* by which his people should live....There is in the New Testament no *Manual of Discipline* like that found in the scrolls of the Dead Sea community....The spiritual discipline of the Christian community is too comprehensive and dynamic to be contained in such a summary of rules. But the lack of a *Manual of Discipline* does not mean that there is no New Testament ordering of the structure of the church. What that order is, how extensive and how universal, these are questions that cannot be answered in advance but only from the New Testament itself."[50]

It is this failure that lies at the heart of Orlando Costas' three-fold problem with the Church Growth school approach. "(1) It militates against the historico-universal character of the church. (2) It makes a universal generalization out of a historical particularity. (3) It makes a theological principle out of a missiological failure."[51]

It is this failure also that will not resolve most of the problems left by early evangelical theorizing regarding the indigenous church. The functional limitation of missions to pioneer evangelism and church

---

[46]Wagner, *Church/Mission Tensions Today,* p. 36.

[47]*Ibid.,* p. 114.

[48]*Ibid.,* pp. 226-227.

[49]*Ibid.,* p. 231. Cf. also Wagner, *Frontiers in Missionary Strategy,* p. 173, for a similar judgment.

[50]Gerber, *op. cit.,* pp. 235-236.

[51]Costas, *op. cit.,* pp. 171-172.

planting remains a problematic presupposition of the school. An avenue for escaping charges of paternalism and colonialistic control remains unopened structurally. The definition of "missionary mission" as discipling in a first-stage isolation from perfecting cannot help but contribute to the let-George-do-it restriction of evangelism to the work of the mission and the subsequent encapsulation which Wagner properly fears as "the church development syndrome."

Biblical Guidelines Toward A Solution

None of this is to say that the classical Reformed formulations of church-mission relationships offer a fully adequate answer. J. H. Bavinck's treatment here is rather typical.

Bavinck is aware of the dangers implicit in distinctions like older and younger churches. Preferring the terms, "mother and daughter churches," he sees the problem as rooted in two alternatives. "Ought the mother church to keep its hands off and leave a young congregation, with its own ministers and consistory, to itself? Or, initially at least, ought the mother church to retain a certain authority, support and guidance?"[52] His own solution is the latter alternative, admitting with it the difficulty of both drawing parallels between the missionary work of the apostolic church and today, and then drawing any conclusions on the basis of supposed parallels. His solution is to resort to what he calls "practical experience."[53]

That experience tells him that in general "younger churches" (his language) at first cannot do without the care of the missionary. He is careful to cite the dangers of such a retention of authority and leadership. Where does the authority of the missionary come from in that church? He is not an apostle and can hardly appeal to Paul as an example. The danger will be that such oversight will keep the young church artifically immature. And again, the missionary will regard himself as indispensable, thus enforcing the immaturity of the church.

Bavinck's treatment has a number of useful insights. He shows great sensitivity to the separating tendency of words like "younger" and "older." He is anxious to reject any idea of an authority which the old church exercises over the younger church, because of its age. "Each church," he says, "which is innerly bound to Jesus Christ and listens to His voice, is as

---

[52]J. H. Bavinck, *An Introduction to the Science of Missions* (Philadelphia: The Presbyterian and Reformed Publ. Comp., 1960), p. 195.
[53] *Ibid.,* p. 196.

such a member of the body of Christ. It is one with all others, no matter where they may be ...."[54] He is also deeply aware of the dangers present in the relation of church to mission and mission to church. So he argues "it is most desirable ... that when an independent church has grown up, the missionary ought to withdraw from its internal affairs and turn its care over to the consistory."[55] This does not mean, for him, a missionary withdrawal to the regions beyond, as Venn argued. "The missionary's job is still important.... He must remain at his post and offer assistance with word and deed, whenever his aid is sought."

Nevertheless, even Bavinck's treatment suffers from many of the fundamental defects of the evangelical circle. (1) Though he repudiates the distinction between older and younger churches, he retains it in his distinction of mother and daughter church. And here the language is even more liable to misunderstanding. At least, "older" and "younger" stressed the chronological element. His language implies even stronger dependence of one on the other. And this presupposition of dependence shows in his failure to avoid totally the older-younger vocabulary. (2) Though he sees the dangers of separating unnaturally the missionary from the new church, he sees no other alternative than the one he cites, namely, the mother church retaining a measure of authority over the daughter church. His own arguments using the relation of the Jerusalem church to the rest of the body of Christ can also be used effectively against his own position.[56] (3) He senses also the problem, with his view of the relation of mother and daughter church, in understanding the authority of the missionary. He realizes that authority for his work does not come from him as an apostle or from any backlog of Christian experience he has with which the "younger church" cannot yet participate. Yet, after admitting this, he goes on to assert and assume that very authority. (4) He continues to assume the givenness of the separate existence of the mission from the church, at least in terms of the presence of the missionary. And here, he is not far from the problems of evangelical thought and the Church Growth school. John Yoder's judgment on the Church Growth school could also be said of Bavinck. "From the point of view of the Believers' Church understanding of the mission of the church, i.e., of the *church as mission;* from the perspective of the conviction that Constantine was a mistake and that the church must refocus her visible structures and faithfulness before the

---

[54] *Ibid.,* pp. 194-195.
[55] *Ibid.,* p. 198.
[56] *Ibid.,* p. 194.

various tasks of the church can go on being done adequately; from the perspective of the view of ministry as the ministry of the total body for the edification of the body as a whole—from these perspectives, I suggest, this peculiar institution of the modern western mission society is subject to some limitations."[57]

Bavinck's arguments suffer from the same fundamental defect of assuming the cultural existence of the mission as separate from the church as a theological principle. He approaches the Scriptures with the presupposition of that operating model. It is precisely here that his discussion of the authority of the missionary fails. It assumes an extra-biblical office and then searches for biblical support to justify that extra-biblical structure.

How then shall we build a biblical theological structure to resolve these problems?

Missionary Nature of the Church

The history of Reformed theorizing about Missions has long recognized the establishment of the church as one of the purposes of Missions. J. H. Bavinck's repetition of that aim in his book is linked to Voetius and Kuyper before him. And yet, conversely, in the classic Reformed formulations of ecclesiology present in the three forms of unity and the Westminster standards, that recognition has not functioned in a normative way. Recently Richard DeRidder has drawn our attention to the rather static and passive place Missions occupies in these creeds. Missing is reflection upon the church's purpose as God's established people in the world, used by God to approach the world He would redeem. "The church becomes only the place where certain things are done...and it is not looked upon as a group which God has called into existence to do something. The marks of the Church need to be placed decisively within the framework of the Church's mission. This is where they were first set, for in Acts 2:42 the teaching, fellowship, breaking of bread, and prayers of the newly-formed Spirit-filled and Spirit-enlarged disciple fellowship is described within the missionary context of the Pentecost story from which it cannot be extracted."[58]

---

[57]Wilbert R. Shenk, editor, *The Challenge of Church Growth* (Elkhart, Ind.: Institute of Memmomite Studies, 1973), p. 41. I take exception to the ambiguity and liability of Yoder's words, "church as mission."

[58]Richard R. De Ridder, *The Dispersion of the People of God* (Kampen: J. K. Kok, 1971), p. 213.

This is not to be understood as some neo-orthodox definition of the church solely in terms of function. We are not saying the church *is* mission. But we are saying the church *has* mission. We are saying the direction of the church is always outward, nets cast into the sea, seeds broadcast, leaven kneaded into the meal, lights for darkness, mustard seeds that grew into shrubs where the birds of heaven may rest.

Our view of the church must be pilgrim enough to shatter the image-making process that restricts missions to the church *there* and not *here,* and re-defines the church invisible as the one to which the missionary belongs, the one which becomes visible once every three to five years at slide presentations. We must re-capture the biblical dimension of the church as the new dispersion of the people of God, sheep scattered when the Shepherd was smitten (Zech. 13:7; Matt. 26:31), gathered again at Jerusalem, and scattered once more till we meet again in the new Jerusalem. As "the twelve tribes who are dispersed abroad" (James 1:1; I Peter 1:1), the church has been called "to proclaim his name among all the nations" (Luke 24:47). We are a race of Abrahams, living in tents "in the land of Promise, as in a foreign land" (Heb. 11:9). We are the children of Israel called to a new wilderness wandering (Isaiah 35:4-9), no longer in isolation from Egypt or Canaan. Now, "all flesh will see it together" (Isaiah 40:5). We are the new Exodus, watching the desert transformed into an orchard (Isaiah 35:7), reaping the eschatological harvest of God (Isaiah 27:12; Joel 3:13; Amos 9:9, 13ff, Luke 10:2). As of old, God will come to be our guide (Ex. 14:19; Psalm 52:12).

That mission is to be undertaken in fellowship, a fellowship of the Spirit (II Cor. 13:14) much more than "partnership of mutuality and equality"[59] or "cooperation of autonomous equals."[60] The one Spirit forms one body through one faith and hope in one God (Eph. 4:4). At Pentecost the Spirit comes as at Sinai with the signs of divine presence and power: the mighty wind, the tongues of flame (Ex. 19:18; 20:18; I Kings 19:11-12; Acts 2:1-3). And as at Sinai he constituted a people to be a kingdom of priests before the nations, so now he constitutes a new people from the four corners of the earth (Acts 2:9-11), to send to the four corners of the earth. Old boundary lines between Israel and Samaria are erased by the reception of the Spirit and the word of the Spirit (Acts 8:14-15). A skeptical Peter is convinced by three visions and the pouring out of the gift of the Spirit on a Roman

[59]Gerber, *op. cit.,* pp. 197 ff.
[60] *Ibid.,* pp. 153 ff.

soldier and returns to the church at Jerusalem with a message: we can no longer call *foreign* what God calls His; we can no longer call Jerusalem *home* in the worldwide fellowship of the Spirit (acts 10-11). One body in one Spirit, with one mission, now marches to the end of the world. Life in the spirit is life in fellowship, and that is much more than simply "equal partnership."

That biblical dimension calls for much more in the relation of foreign mission and national church than simply consultative relation of modified fusion. Pluriformist distinctions of sodalities and modalities, mother and daughter churches, continue a pattern not fully biblical. Peter's "church development syndrome" was not cured simply by a call to evangelize Cornelius, but also by a reminder that the fellowship of the Spirit calls nothing home or foreign (Acts 10:15). Surely, the Reformation emphasis on the catholicity of the church demands structural changes that will reflect that catholicity.

In the awesome complexity of transition, between the initiation of evangelistic work in an area, and the forming of the structure of the church, the patterns implicit in terminology like "partnership of mutuality" and "cooperation of autonomous equals" are serviceable,[61] as much as in the transition of a North American home mission work from preaching point to formal organization as a structured body of Christ. But ultimately, the biblical call to unity in the worldwide fellowship Christ instituted is a call to the consideration of the legitimacy of separate structures. It calls us to a consideration of the internationalization of missions on the denominational level, the presence on our North American Foreign Mission Boards of brothers from Korea and Nigeria for evaluating gifts and priorities, a structural means of fellowship between denominations here and there that will be more of a world synod than a world council. It calls us to a consideration of the continued legitimacy of Missions existing "separate but equal" with national sister churches on the field. It calls us to examine radically any structure that by its existence or form hinders the full expression of that unity of fellowship and service that is the full, ordered

---

[61]I see no particularly sharp difference between these concepts. As Edwin Jacques has commented regarding their use at Green Lake, "when the dust had settled, few persons could distinguish any significant difference between the two positions. Both mission and church were to maintain their separate identity and organization" ("An Equal Partnership Structure," *Evangelical Missions Quarterly*, Vol. 9, No. 2, 1973, p. 65).

life of the people of God, the body of Christ, the fellowship of the Spirit.[62]

Missionary Office in the Church

In the missionary form of the church, goals are not oriented simply on the world and not the church, but first of all to God in worship, and, in that ministry, to the people of God and to the world. God formed His people at Sinai that they might serve Him in worship (Exod. 19:6-7), and He continues to form His people for the same purpose. "Ye are an elect race, a royal priesthood, a holy nation, a people for God's own possession, that ye may show forth the excellencies of him who called you out of darkness into his marvellous light" (I Peter 2:9).

Worship itself becomes witness, part of God's campaign against "the church development syndrome." The giving of the Spirit at Pentecost equips the church with new tongues to glorify God before the nations for His mighty works (Acts 2:11). Paul sees the Old Testament promises of the nations celebrating God's praises as God's people (Psalm 107.21,22; Isaiah 2:2-4; Zech. 8:22-23) partially fulfilled in his apostolic ministry of "offering up the Gentiles" (Rom. 15:16). Whether this refers to the Gentiles as presenting an offering, or being themselves that offering, Paul's view of missions is conceived as worship to God, fruit of praise offered from the lips of the Gentiles (Rom. 15:9-11), "tribute" brought to God by Gentile benevolence. (Rom. 15:6, 25, 26).

In the structure of the church, "witness to the world cannot be isolated as the ministry of the church, nor even as the primary ministry of the church. On the other hand, it does not follow that witness to the world is subordinate, or optional—a goal to be sought only after the church has been at great pains to take care of itself."[63] For when that ministry to the world is neglected, worship is emasculated, and edification becomes indoctrination. "But when the church in obedience to Christ seeks to make disciples of the nations, then worship rises up: men cry out in prayer for boldness and for doors of opportunity (Acts 4:29; Col. 4:3; Eph. 6:19), the praises of the newly converted join with the thanksgiving of the saints. The

---

[62]It is disappointing to see the otherwise excellent analysis of Orlando Costas and his appeal to go beyond the structural dichotomy of church and mission to church *in* mission and with little more than pointing to the Latin American Community of Evangelical Ministries as an integrative attempt at re-structuring along his suggested lines *(op. cit.,* pp. 173-174). Highly commendable though that example may be, the structure still remains a "sodality" and less than ideal.

[63]Gerber, *op. cit.,* p. 278.

church is edified together in obedient service, each member ministering to make the others more fruitful contributors to the whole ministry of the church."[64]

Is Dr. George Peters right in suggesting that our missionary thrust must be to the world and not to the church,[65] if we are to overcome the dual administration of church and mission which he sees as "a principal cause of tension in many fields"?[66]

If missions is the work of the church, then the work of missions must be the church, not only "church-based" but also "church-faced." The New Testament figure of the body of Christ, in fact, has that specialized focus. It is never used to describe the ministry of the church to the world but always to picture the mutuality of the ministry of Christians to Christians in the church. The gifts of the Spirit are oriented "for the perfecting of the saints, unto the work of ministering, unto the building up of the body of Christ" (Eph. 4:11-16). Even the unique and unrepeatable ministry of the apostolate was exercised partially in returning to Lystra, Iconium and Derbe, "confirming the souls of the disciples" (Acts 14:21-22), not simply planting churches but strengthening them in the faith (Acts 16:5). And evangelists like Timothy and Titus found themselves in a ministry directed to the church at places like Thessalonica (Acts 17), Ephesus (I Tim. 1:3) and Crete (Titus 1:5). We are given to the church as stewards (I Cor. 3:21-23). The mission to the building up of the church has a central place in the New Testament picture of stewardship in office (I Cor. 12:4-31; Rom. 12:3-7).

That ministry, however church-faced, need not be church-captivated in the syndrome Peters properly fears — "perfecting church structures, drafting constitutions, exercising church discipline, and superintending institutions."[67] For gifts given for the mission of the church set the scope of one's service (Eph. 4:7). And these gifts are as diverse as the structures of ministry among the new people of God. The first place given by the New Testament to gifts associated with the ministry of the Word (I Cor. 12:8, 28; Rom. 12:6,7) may not be reduced by waiting on tables (Acts 6:2, 4), or superintending institutions. But neither may missionaries with gifts for governing function (Rom. 12:8; I Tim. 5:17) avoid rule in the church, lest they be guilty of quenching the Spirit by refusing to use the talents given by God (I Thess. 5:19). Leadership in the community of the Spirit is not determined by nationality or which side of the water the steward of gifts

---

[64] *Ibid.*, p. 279.

[65] *Ibid.*, p. 216.

[66] McGavran, *op. cit.*, p. 10.

[67] Gerber, *op. cit.*, p. 208.

calls home, but by the community's recognition of those gifts in its midst (Acts 1:23, 6:3). A missionary may not usurp a role for which he does not have gifts (Rom. 12:3; II Cor. 10:13), nor may he spurn a role in the church for which he does have gifts (Rom. 1:14). His role in the church is always determined by his gifts, not by his nationality.

Must mission in isolation from the church focus its priorities on evangelism, not on service? To do so can come close to isolating institutionally all that "Jesus began to do" from all that "Jesus began to teach" (Acts 1:1), forgetting the integrity of ministry offered to God, to the church, and to the world. Worship offered to God is not heard when it is offered by "hands...full of blood" (Isaiah 1:11-16). Missions that seek to serve God must also "relieve the oppressed, judge the fatherless, plead for the widow" (Isaiah 1:17). We may not ask, "Who is the church's neighbor?" or, "Who is the mission's neighbor?" But simply, "Who is my neighbor?" (Luke 10:29). "Where the love of God rules and every man cares for the things of others a ministry of compassion must flourish. In the ministry of Jesus, the signs of kingdom power were deeds of mercy: Christ healed the sick and fed the hungry."[68] Any structural differentiation, any allotment of priorities of function, that obstructs that integrity of Christian love in word and deed (James 2:15-16) must be questioned.

Again, this is not to say that a ministry to widows may sidetrack those whose gifts and calling require them to "continue steadfastly in prayer and in the ministry of the word" (Acts 6:2, 4)), church planters becoming hospital administrators, evangelists becoming seminary teachers.

Nor does it mean that a mission, in whatever stage of integration it may have achieved with the national church acts with wisdom, in the face of a large non-Christian population and an existent church however small, by seeking for a preponderance of men with gifts for the ministries of mercy and order and not for men with gifts for evangelism. With the sober judgment of a steward, we must remember that the use of gifts in the body "often includes the *where* as well as the *when* of Christian service. The church recognized that the gifts granted to Peter and Paul distinguished the area of their ministry. Both had full apostolic authority, but one was sent particularly to the Jews and the other to the Gentiles (Gal. 2:7-10)"[69] Paul's

---

[68] *Ibid.,* p. 282.

[69] Edmund P. Clowney, *Called To The Ministry* (Philadelphia: Westminster Theological Seminary, 1964), p. 87.

own judgments, in concert with his fellow workers, as to the expressed needs of the churches played a part in the stewardship of his own gifts (Phil. 2:12, 19-25; II Cor. 1:15-23). That same stewardship may properly function in evaluating strategic priorities of ministry on the field. We are arguing simply that they must be ordered and function in the whole body of Christ in that area.

Discipline of Gifts in the Church

Order and structure in the body of Christ is necessary for the regulation of ardor (I Cor. 14:40), but it cannot create it. And a loosely decentralized structure comes no closer to solving the problem of either the discipline of gifts or their creation.[70] In fact, in terms of discipline, it cannot help but be less fruitful.

But it is in the discipline of gifts in the body that many of the most basic tensions in church-mission relations appear. Wagner has asserted that "when missionaries are out on the growing edge, bringing unbelievers to Christ, organizing them into congregations, and handing over the new churches to the denomination, few national leaders are going to tell *that* kind of missionary to go home."[71] But when even that kind of missionary labors with a patent colonialism, an abrasive paternalism or a self-assertive egotism, he will be as unwelcome as the missionary uninterested in church planting. And when the national church with which he labors is a bureaucratic institution whose mission interest is directed by church politicians building a power base through the use of mission funds and structure, the tensions will remain. For this reason, Green Lake focused so much of its attention on problems of mutual trust and respect.

The insistence at Green Lake by some "that spiritual and personal problems were...fundamental and serious" was well taken.[72] Their equal insistence that they were "much more fundamental and serious" than questions of structure forgets the reason for structure in the church — the discipling of gifts of the Spirit in the fellowship of the Spirit, the church. The bifurcation of church and mission institutionally does not allow the Reformation mark of the church to be fully operative in the resolution of the dilemma.

---

[70]David Cho, in the Lausanne volume, *Let the Earth Hear His Voice,* pleads for such a decentralized structure *(op. cit.,* pp. 501-507). His plea does not seem to have an adequate awareness of either of these two dimensions.

[71]Wagner, *op. cit.,* p. 171.

[72]Wagner, *Church/Mission Tensions Today,* p. 36.

The corrective for paternalism in the missionary is his recognition of the "paternalism" of God in his Son, Jesus Christ. Authority in the church is resident in Christ's mediatorial authority (Matthew 28:18; Phil. 2:9-11). The authority of pastor, evangelist, elder and deacon, national or foreign, flows from "grace given" (Rom. 1:5, 12:3; I Cor. 3:10), from the enduements of an enthroned Christ (Eph. 4:7-8). The missionary and the national churchman alike are stewards, not colonialistic lords or bureaucratic bosses (Tit. 1:7; I Cor. 4:1-4; I Pet. 4:10-11). They are ministers, not masters (I Pet. 5:3). The symbols of their authority are not budgets but towels (John 13:12-16). Discipline begins here in the body.

The corrective for lack of trust in one another lies in the recognition by missionary and churchman that the variety of their gifts for ministry serves the unity of the body. The mutuality of gifts must unite missions and church in the bearing of one another's burdens, in the gentle restoration of those overtaken in sin (Gal. 6:1-2), in the exclusion of those who defile the fellowship by sin (Matt. 18:8, 17-20; Rom. 16:17). The gifts of the missionary must edify the body and the other gifts of the body must edify him. The *body* grows in the image of Christ the Head through the proper functioning of each part: "till we all attain...unto a fullgrown man" (Eph. 4:11-16). And that growth takes place as nothing is done "through faction or vainglory, but in lowliness of mind each esteems others better than himself" (Phil. 2:3).

As long as mission and church, missionary and national church, are isolated from one another in separate structures, that communal exercise of mutual encouragement and discipline in one body will be handicapped though not impossible. The search for some biblical justification for the exercise of missionary authority in the national church will remain fruitless, severed as it is institutionally from the New Testament norm that "a man cannot normally exercise authority in the church until that authority has been recognized by the church."[73] The only full ministry of the body to which the missionary is committed exists some 6000 miles away from where he may labor five out of six years.

---

[73]Gerber, *op. cit.*, p. 284.

CHAPTER EIGHT

THE MISSIONARY FLAME OF REFORMED THEOLOGY

by Edmund P. Clowney*

In a recent textbook of the church growth movement[1] "predestinarianism" is blamed for the lack of church growth at the time of the Reformation. As a shocking example of the way a predestinarian can cut the nerve of church growth John Calvin is quoted, "We are taught that the kingdom of Christ is neither to be advanced nor maintained by the industry of men, but this is the work of God alone."

The origin of the quotation is not given; the difficulty in tracing it is that there are so many passages in the Bible in which we are taught this. It is therefore hard to say which one Calvin was referring to when he used that favorite formula "we are taught."

One might think, for example, of the parable of the seed growing secretly (Mark 64:26ff), but in his comment on that passage Calvin exhorts ministers of the Word to greater diligence in sowing the seed of the gospel since they may trust in God's blessing to add fruit to their labors.

The whole Bible bears God's own witness that salvation is of the Lord, that apart from the new birth of the Spirit a man cannot even see the kingdom of God, much less enter it. Paul's cry of joy in the predestinating

Edmund P. Clowney currently serves as President of Westminster Theological Seminary and Professor of Practical Theology. He came to that post in 1952 after a pastoral ministry in Connecticut, Illinois and New Jersey. Author and contributor to a number of volumes, he played a significant part in the discussions on church-mission relationships at Green Lake, Wisconsin in 1971.

---

[1]Tetsunao Yamamori, E. LeRoy Lawson, *Introducing Church Growth* (Cincinnati, Ohio: Standard Publishing Co., 1975) p. 26. The quotation is taken from J. Herbert Kane, *A Global View of Christian Missions from Pentecost to the Present* (Grand Rapids; Baker Book House, 1971), p. 74.

will of God sums up the history of salvation: "For of him, and through him, and to him, are all things:to whom be glory for ever. Amen" (Rom. 11:36).

Reformed theologians have not learned enough from the great apostle to the Gentiles, but they and the whole church of the reformation have rightly shared Paul's vision of the triumph of God's electing grace in salvation. The problem is not how to reduce or adapt Calvinistic theology to a theology of missions; rather the problem lies in explaining how those who had been so inflamed by the New Testament theology of grace could have so quenched the missionary fire that it kindles.

But our most pressing task is not to analyze the past but to look to the future. What is the missionary flame of Reformed theology? What hope does it bring in the confusion and challenge of Christian mission in the last decades of this century?

The Reformers called the church back to the Word of God where the gospel of grace is proclaimed. Today we must follow their example: no doubt the Reformation too needs reforming if we will subject everything to the authority of the Holy Spirit who has spoken in the Scripture and opens our ears to hear. But we are not surprised to discover that as we search the Scriptures we renew our grasp on those great truths that mastered those who searched the Scriptures before us.

Four of those themes burn within us as we reflect on the world mission of Christ's church in our day: the glory of God, the grace of God, the kingdom of God, and the Word of God. Each has rich meaning for our understanding of the Gospel and our obedience to it. There is no separate theology of missions to be added to Reformed theology as an appendix, but there is a missionary depth and heart to the very doctrines that are most precious and central to the Reformed faith.

The Glory of God The Goal of Missions

We may begin by looking at the end — the climax of Paul's doxology and the final purpose of God's plan of salvation, and indeed of all things — the glory of God. "For of him, and through him, and unto him are all things. To him be the glory for ever. Amend" (Rom. 11:36).

Paul writes in awe as he reflects on the divine mystery, the theology of the mission of God. No mission problem was more acute for the apostle than his calling to proclaim the gospel among the Gentiles. Daily he bore the reproach of being a renegade, of betraying his own people to curry favor with the heathen. He was driven to reflect on the ways of the Lord as he saw his own people rejecting their Messiah and the Gentiles entering by faith into the number of the true people of God. The answer given to Paul by the inspiration of the Spirit is a magnificent vision of the purpose of God revealed across the panorama of the history of redemption in the Old Testament. Israel was called to worship God; in the fullness of God's blessing on Israel the nations would be summoned to hear and join in the praises of Zion. The seed of Abraham would be blessed so abundantly that they would be made a blessing to the ends of the earth.

But Israel failed in this mission. Through disobedience the people of God brought upon themselves judgment rather than blessing. Jerusalem was destroyed; the cloud of glory was exchanged for the smoke of burning and the disobedient nation was taken into captivity. Yet the idolatry that brought destruction on Israel was not the final apostasy. Restored from captivity and purged from idolatry a remnant took up the law of God with zeal — zeal that Paul the Pharisee shared with his teachers. In that zeal to establish their own righteousness they rejected the righteousness of God. Faced with the claim of Jesus to be the Messiah and the Son of God they joined in his crucifixion. Paul's own hands were red with the blood of Christ's disciples.

Was there nothing left but the wrath of God against the wicked husbandmen who killed the son that the inheritance might be theirs (Matt. 21:33-43)?

Against that dreadful conclusion Paul could set the amazing grace of the Messiah Jesus toward him. On the road to Damascus Jesus had arrested him in the full fury of persecuting zeal and claimed him as his apostle to fulfill the calling of the seed of Abraham by declaring Christ's name before the kings of the nations (Acts 9:15, 16). On the road to Damascus Paul's eyes were blinded by the *glory* of the Lord; Paul's ministry was a ministry of glory—not, of course, his own glory, for Paul, the chief of sinners, persecuting the church, had nothing to glory of in. All that he might glory in he had learned to count as refuse that he might again Christ (Phil. 3:8). "He that glorieth, let him glory in the Lord!" (I Cor. 1:31). The glory of Paul's ministry was the glory of God in the face of Jesus Christ. The glory of God is not an abstract principle for the apostle, but the purpose of every day's labor in his mission.

Paul understood that the Lord who chose to be glorified in him is the Lord who works all things according to the counsel of his will. He has not cast off his people whom he foreknew. There remains a remnant according to God's electing grace. Paul himself — by God's free grace — is included in that remnant. Moreover, God's dealings with Israel and the nations in the past hold the clue to his purposes of mercy in the present. When Israel was judged of old, blessing flowed to the Gentiles, not simply in spite of Israel's failure, but as a result of God's judgment upon that failure. Naaman is blessed and preserved to be a scourge of Israel; Hazael is annointed king of Syria to bring judgment; Ninevah is spared to carry Israel into captivity. So then, in Paul's day, when branches are broken off the olive tree of the people of God, the Gentiles as wild olive branches are grafted in. But the story cannot end there. God is able to graft in again the natural branches and Paul ministers the gospel to the Gentiles in the fervent hope that as they enter into the blessings of the kingdom of God, the sons of the kingdom may be aroused to jealousy and come streaming in — not merely the *remnant* of Israel being gathered with the remnant of the nations as the prophets had promised, but the *fullness* of Israel and of the Gentiles — the great host that makes up the full number of the elect people of God. "For as ye in time past were disobedient to God, but now have obtained mercy by their disobedience, even so have these also now been disobedient, that by the mercy shown to you they also may now obtain mercy" (Rom. 11:30).

These are the profound meditations that move Paul to adore the sovereign grace of God's plan of salvation. In his missionary task he is leading in the worship of God. In the fifteenth chapter of Romans he describes his whole apostolic mission in these terms. He would remind the Romans "of the grace that was given me of God, that I should be a minister of Christ Jesus unto the Gentiles, ministering the gospel of God, that the offering up of the Gentiles might be made acceptable, being sanctified by the Holy Spirit. I have therefore my glorying in Christ Jesus in things pertaining to God" (Rom. 15:15c-17).

The great offering of the Gentiles Paul sees as the fulfillment of the prophecies of Isaiah (Isa. 56:7; 60:7, 66:20). After the Suffering Servant has been despised and rejected of men (Isa. 53:3), he is exalted by God and in that resurrection exaltation all the promises of God find their fulfillment. In spite of Israel's disobedience the promises to Abraham are realized, for "Christ hath been made a minister of the circumcision for the truth of God, that he might confirm the promises given unto the fathers, and that the Gentiles might glorify God for his mercy" (Rom. 15:8, 9).

Gentiles who had been barred from God's altar are now led in by the apostle, to offer not the sacrifices of bulls and goats, but their bodies as living sacrifices in the spiritual temple composed of living stones (cf. Rom. 12:1, 2; Eph. 2:22; I Pet. 2:5). The songs of Gentile praise ascend to God as the prophets and psalmists had promised (Rom. 15:9-12; Ps. 18:49;

Deut. 32:43; Isa. 11:10), and Paul, the apostle to the Gentiles, ministers in this great service of worship by the preaching of the gospel.[2]

Further, Paul's gospel ministry is drawn into the most immediate union and fellowship with the Lord he serves. Christ himself is a minister of the circumcision, not in the sense that he ministers to them but in the sense that he takes up their ministry. He is the true Israel of God, God's Son and God's Servant, Heir of all the promises of God and the only Mediator of God's saving mercies. As the minister of the circumcision Jesus Christ sings to the name of the Father among the Gentiles, leading in the praises of God in the assembly of his brethren gathered from the nations (Rom. 15:9).

The goal and fulfillment of the saving mission of the Son is that the name of the Father might be glorified in the eternal song of the redeemed (Rev. 15:3, 4).

Now, we may ask, what practical result does this exalted aim have in dealing with the concrete problems of missions today? Does it change our perspective with reference to church growth? Does it offer guidance on the demand for a moratorium on North American and European missionaries? Does it direct us with respect to political implications of the missionary message?

We face a real danger in considering these questions. The danger lies in supposing that what changes everything does not really change anything. Surely a deeper devotion to the glory of God must strengthen all the mission of the church in the world, but, we are tempted to think, it can have no direct bearing on the immediate problems we face. Every Christian really knows better. How often has the pattern of our own lives been radically changed when we were confronted with the call to do *all* to the glory of God. We found that the goal of God's glory was not a remote end, like a point in infinity, toward which any line of life might be extended. Rather, we discovered that an eye single to the glory of God altered our daily conduct in every particular. Even the common actions of life that we repeated took on a different style as well as a different context and meaning.

How searching the doxological theme of missions becomes as God's Spirit applies it to our missionary practice! How it demolishes the empire-building of our missionary organizations! What transformations of missionary labor would result from a genuine and whole-hearted desire to

---

[2]Paul calls himself a "liturgete" *leitourgos* of Christ Jesus to the Gentiles, ministering as a priest *hierourgounta* the gospel of God (Rom. 15:16).

hear the nations singing God's praise with the Savior in their midst! Are national churches seeking Christ's praise in asserting their right to separate development? Or do the songs of political freedom rise above the hosannas of the people of God?

In our efforts to strengthen the cause of missions are we aiming at God's glory or at worldly success? Jesus ministered to great multitudes, but they were progressively alienated by his message and they left him to die alone on the cross — that death in which God was supremely glorified.

Surely the doxological goal of missions must serve first the purpose of heart searching. Yet we dare not ignore its implications for the issues in debate.

On the one hand there is the sobering realization that God's name is vindicated and his glory revealed in his judgments as well as in his blessings. Paul clearly reflects on this, not only in Romans 9-11 but in the whole epistle. The revelation of the righteousness of God preached by Paul has two sides — the justifying righteousness that is the gift of God's grace through faith in Jesus Christ and the retributive righteousness that is God's judgment, also given to Jesus Christ (Rom. 1:17, 18). Jesus came to Nazareth to preach, not because he judged the Nazarenes to be "winnable," but because the glory of God demanded that the gospel declaration be made in the town where Christ was brought up. Paul's repeated preaching in the synagogues was not a policy pragmatically determined by its success nor was it a means of recruiting Gentile proselytes of Judaism to serve as the nucleus for a Christian congregation. Rather Paul presented the gospel to the Jew first in order to honor the promises and plan of God, even if the result was a witness against the rebellious to be remembered in the day of judgment (Acts 13:46-47).

On the other hand, Jesus declares that his Father is glorified when his disciples bear much fruit (John 15:8). In his work of creation God put man in a fruitful garden and charged him to be fruitful and multiply. In his work of redemption God plants his vineyard in prepared ground, hedges, cultivates, and watches over it that it may bear much fruit (Isa. 5:1-7). If fruit is not borne, the vine is subject to the pruning of chastening and ultimately to the burning of outpoured wrath (Isa. 5; Jer. 2:21; Ezek 15:1-8; 19:10-14; Matt. 21:33-45; John 15:6). To be sure, fruit-bearing in the New Testament is itself defined in terms of glorifying God (with the fruit of our lips, Heb. 13:15), growing in holiness and love (John 15:2), and ministering to the saints (Rom. 1:13; Phil. 1:22; Phil. 4:17). But good works cause God's name to be glorified by those who see them (Matt. 5:16), and the disciples chosen by Jesus to bear much fruit (John 15:16) are sent in his name to the nations. Christ glorified the Father in his death, and by the lifting up of his death and exaltation he will draw all men unto himself (John 12:32). He is the grain of wheat falling into the earth alone in his death, but bearing much fruit in his resurrection (John 12:24). God is glorified as the fields white to the harvest are reaped, as the nets full to breaking are drawn in, as the great host that no man can number sings the praises of the Father in the name of the Lamb. The fruit that God seeks is given in the True Vine, Jesus Christ: of him our fruit is found (cf. Hos. 14:4-8), He is the Messiah, the Branch, and he drinks the wine of his death on the cross that we might produce the wine of his resurrection fruitfulness in newness of life.

To seek the glory of the Father is to have fellowship in the mission of the Son, who could rejoice that the mysteries of the kingdom were hidden from the wise and prudent and revealed unto babes, for so it was well pleasing in the Father's sight (Luke 10:21). But that same Son of God pointed his disciples to the harvest and called them to be fishers of men only after he had filled their nets with fish. Men may prefer a simpler or more one-sided motivation, but Jesus knew the awesome glory of his Father's sovereign grace and reflected that glory in all of his ministry.

The doxological mode in missions goes beyond a certain optimism in the expectation of response. Rather it praises God for the assurance of the gathering in of all the sheep of Christ into the eternal fold. The Psalms celebrate God's triumphs, past, present, and future, and summon the nations to join in the song. The new song of the church of Christ celebrates his resurrection triumph in the hallelujahs of heaven begun on earth. "But ye are an elect race, a royal priesthood, a holy nation, a people for God's own possession, that he may show forth the excellencies of him who called you out of darkness into his marvelous light" (I Pet. 2:9). In a world of death, the church sings the joy of Christ's resurrection; in a world of despair, the church sings the sure hope of Christ's return. You may have smiled at the sound-track on a TV drama. If the heroine could only hear the swelling coda of the last few minutes she would know that the hero was riding down the last slope to the triumph of their reunion. The church needs to hear the sound-track in the drama of the returning Lord; she would then not be tempted to abandon her sure hope for the open-ended dialogue of another talk show.

The Grace of God the Source of Missions

The doxology of missions is a rainbow of praise arching over the throne of God. The end of that rainbow is the glory of God but its beginning is the grace of God. If all things are unto him, all things must also be of him. All is *to* God's glory because all is *of* God's grace.

The Bible records, not man's search for God, but God's search for man. The initiative in salvation is always his. God calls to Adam in the garden after man's first transgression, and God seeks for worshipers in the whole history of redemption—calling Abraham out of Ur, coming down the stairway of grace to Jacob, calling Moses at the burning bush, David in the sheepfold, Isaiah in the temple. Jesus grounds his final mission in his Father's electing purpose. He has other sheep that are not of this fold, and them also he must bring. They are his sheep because they have been given him of the Father; they are his because he gives his life for them. He must and will bring them, for they will hear his voice (John 10:27). God's choosing of his sheep and God's drawing them to his Son (John 6:44) are the basis in Christ's own understanding for his death on the cross and his lifting up to glory.

Jesus not only rests in the mystery of God's electing grace; he rejoices in it. "I thank thee, O Father, Lord of heaven and earth, that thou didst hide these things from the wise and understanding, and didst reveal them unto babes: yea, Father, for so it was well-pleasing in thy sight" (Matt. 11:25, 26).

The high mystery of God's choosing of his own in Christ before the foundation of the world (Eph. 1:3-5) silences us with wonder. This scriptural doctrine is subject to constant and railing attack by those who judge it with the mind of the flesh. Sadly, it is sometimes defended in a strangely similar manner. But God has a purpose in drawing aside the veil, in permitting us to hear the very prayer of the Song to the Father. The purpose is that we might not glory in ourselves but in the mercy of our saving God. Significantly, the Word of God does not present God's electing grace as a barrier but as an encouragement to mission. When Paul is tempted to leave Corinth in discouragement Christ appears to him in a vision to inform him, "I have much people in this city" (Acts 18:10). Christ's other sheep were not at that point evident to the apostle, but the fact that the Lord's elect were to be found in that seamy and sophisticated seaport gave Paul assurance in continuing his mission. Because Christ's grace is sovereign, it is sure. The elect are not always evident: Elijah was not aware of seven thousand who had not bowed the knee to Baal (I Kings 19:18).

Jesus' sign of the miraculous catch of fish was given to disciples who had fished all night and caught nothing. They might have refused Jesus' command to let down their nets on the ground that the lake had been exhaustively water-tested and the absence of catchable fish pragmatically established. Peter seems to have wavered for a moment before he said, "Nevertheless, at thy word, I will let down the nets" (Luke 5:5).

Dealing with those who refuse the gospel is one thing. The time comes when the heralds of the kingdom must shake off the dust of their feet against those who will not hear the message (Matt. 10:14). But precisely because God's election is gracious and sure we dare not categorize populations as devoid of God's elect. To be sure, advocates of church growth have not proposed in principle that we abandon resistant populations, but only that we put a higher priority on efforts to reach receptive populations. Nevertheless, to suggest that the presence or absence of God's elect in a people can be determined by sample receptivity to the gospel overlooks the biblical emphasis on the hiddenness of God's elect. Indeed, even receptivity may be misleading. Because Jesus knew men's hearts he did not trust himself to the enthusiasm of the crowd that professed to believe in his name (John 2:23-25).

The Calvinistic preacher who told William Carey that if God willed the conversion of the heathen he could do it without Carey's help[3] gives us a dismaying example of how to abuse a biblical truth by an unbiblical application. The biblical doctrine of election cannot be used to excuse our disobedience to Christ's missionary command. Neither can it be used to provide heavenly endorsement for our strategic planning. It remains as God's witness to his sovereignty; it humbles all our pride and offers another assurance — the assurance of the triumph of God's will and God's way in the full ingathering of his harvest.

But if church growth writers in their zeal for evangelism have sometimes been tempted to computerize God's election they have rightly resisted the universalism of contemporary theology which would vaporize God's election by making it unquantifiable. The universalist position is persuasively argued by those who claim that election is solely to service. They maintain that the election church is the servant church. It does not differ from the world by being a company of the saved, an ark of the redeemed floating in a sea of perdition; rather, it differs not in status but in

---

[3]F. Deaville Walker, *William Carey, Missionary Pioneer and Statesman* (Chicago: Moody Press, 1960), p. 54.

function. The church is chosen to announce to the world that every man is elect in Christ.

On this assumption the ground of election is serviceability. Missionary as this theology may appear in terminology, it destroys the real meaning of missionary endeavor. God's calling is not just to service but to sonship. God redeems his people from bondage in Egypt that he might bear them on eagle's wings to himself (Exod. 19:4). The mystery of God's electing love cannot be explained in terms of some ulterior motive. God tells Israel that he has not chosen them because they are more in number than other people No, he has set his love upon them because...he loves them! (Deut. 7:7, 8). Even in the personal relationship of human love we may have learned that a declaration of love is not necessarily improved by a description of useful qualities in the beloved! In the case of God's love for us, *all* is of grace. God has set his people upon his heart, written their names upon his hands, rejoiced over them as a bridegroom over a bride. He chooses them not simply or finally to use them, but to posssess them — that he might be their God and they his people.

God's free grace, God's sure grace, is the fountain of salvation, a stream without tributaries flowing from his throne of mercy. But God's grace not only has a fixed point of origin with him. It also has a fullness that is of him: the fountain of grace becomes a river flood of mercy. That is, God does not only plan salvation in electing grace; he also executes his plan. In the fullness of time God's grace *triumphs* in a way that surpasses anything we could imagine. At the cross of Calvary God gave his only begotten Son to accomplish the mission of his love.

When the Galatians were tempted to improve on God's free grace by adding their own earned righteousness, Paul cried, "O foolish Galatians, who did bewitch you, before whose eyes Jesus Christ was openly set forth crucified?" (Gal. 3:1). Unlike his legalistic opponents, Paul gloried in the cross. Apostolic mission theology preaches Christ crucified. Contemporary theologies of mission must be tested by that apostolic zeal. The triumph of God's grace at the cross is still the despair of every humanist. To the Jews the cross was a stumbling block, and to the Greeks, foolishness (I Cor. 1:23). How can the arrest, torture, and death of Jesus be regarded as God's victory rather than as his defeat? Only when the cross is seen as God sees it and as Jesus takes it. Paul preached Christ crucified as the Sin-Bearer, the one who was made to be sin for us that we might be made the righteousness of God in him (II Cor. 5:21). Only if sin, not suffering, is the fundamental human problem does the cross bring salvation. The cross is a *triumph* of

God's grace because God gave his only begotten Son to die in the place of sinners.

At the cross the measure of God's love is revealed in the price that the Father paid. All the love of the Father through eternity is given to his beloved Son, the Son of his bosom (John 1:18). The Father so loves the Son that he gives him the world (John 3:35). Nothing that the Son asks of the Father will be refused. Yet in the mystery of God's saving love he gives his only begotten Son for a sinful world. Confused and overwhelmed by that mystery (can the Father love sinners more than his Son?) we can only say that grace means that God loves guilty sinners more than himself. The Son of the Father willingly gives himself, laying down his life for his friends. Yet the Father also gives his Son — and if he delivers him up for us all, "how shall he not with him also freely give us all things?" (Rom. 8:32).

The gospel of the cross presents salvation from eternal death to eternal life accomplished by Christ on Calvary; the Good Shepherd gives his life for the sheep.

When the gospel is secularized or politicized it is simply destroyed. The Lord of love calls us to take up our cross and follow him. Those who call men in Christ's name must promise what he promised: persecution, hatred, family strife, suffering — and eternal life.

Jesus said, "And I, if I be lifted up, will draw all men unto me" (John 12:32). John tells us that the "lifting up" of which Jesus spoke was the lifting up to the cross, the lifting up of his death. Our zeal to reach the lost in our generation springs from the conviction that men are eternally lost without Christ, and that the crucified and risen Christ draws them by faith to himself.

If we follow the New Testament we will perceive the harmony of the crucifixion and the resurrection of Christ in the theme of the saving triumph of God's grace.

The crucified, risen, ascended Christ is the Lord who sends his disciples to the nations. The Spirit he gives is the inbreathing of his own risen life and power (John 20:22). Because Christ's victory is accomplished, the fulfillment of his purposes is not only assured in the future but realized in the present. Just as the Christian's victory over sin is gained by appropriating the finished work of Christ — because we *are* raised with Christ, we walk in newsness of life — so, too the mission of the church is fulfilled by *faith* as the church recognizes and acts upon the reality of Christ's present authority and dominion in heaven and earth. "Go ye *therefore,* and make disciples of all nations...." The gift of the Spirit as the *promise* of the Father not only provides power for witnessing but also seals the actuality of the fulfillment of God's purpose in extending saving blessing to the nations. The doctrines of grace are not only the key to the sanctification of the believer, they are the key to the evangelization of the world. That is because grace and faith forever go together. We triumph over the bondage of sin in our lives as we recognize what Jesus Christ has accomplished in our place on the cross and on the throne; we triumph over the bondage of sin in the world as we recognize that what Jesus Christ has accomplished on the cross and the throne redeems all his people from every nation. The distorting of this truth in the unbiblical universalism of "ecumenical" theology must not blind us to the biblical universalism of Christ's resurrection triumph. The saints will one day judge angels and although they are made a spectacle to angels and men their work has cosmic significance, for by his messengers Jesus Christ wills to gather in the fullnes of Jews and Gentiles — his elect from every tribe, tongue, people, and nation. He is the Prince and Savior, who sovereignly gives repentance to Israel and remission of sins. Paul's opponents argued that his doctrine of justification by faith would lead to license rather than holiness. Paul knew better. Faith reckons to be true what *is* true: when Christ died, we died; when he rose, we rose. So, too, Paul's doctrines have been seen as a threat to missions. But we should know better. Because Christ has ascended on high he has led captivity captive. Reformed missions reckons that to be true which *is* true. Christ is Prince and Savior. He has all power in heaven and earth, and nothing can separate him from those the Father has given him. He sends us to summon those whom he will bring — those other sheep who must be brought to the one flock, the one Shepherd.

The sovereign, triumphant grace by which Christ draws men to himself puts its demand upon us who are trophies of that grace. Christ's total power in heaven and earth assures his disciples of the success of their mission but it also binds them to that mission. "Go ye therefore...." What the disciples are to teach as they go to the nations are the meaning and purposes of that very kingdom in which Jesus is exalted.

The ethics taught by Jesus Christ are the ethics of that kingdom. Jesus' ethical teaching is not something apart from his mission. We cannot tack on a theology of missions to a New Testament theology that has very different concerns. Jesus teaches the theology of the kingdom that is the rationale and support of the mission mandate.

What is the first and great commandment, according to the teaching of

Jesus Christ? To love God with all our heart, soul, strength, and might. The second is "like unto it:" to love our neighbor as ourselves. But what kind of love fulfills God's law? The scribal lawyer who asked Jesus, "Who is my neighbor?" showed by his question that he did not understand the meaning of love. He was thinking in terms of self-righteousness: How could he reduce the commandment to love to manageable proportions so that he could handle its requirements? Jesus told the parable of the Good Samaritan to reverse the lawyer's question. The question is not "Whom must I acknowledge as my neighbor?" Rather it is "To whom may I *be* a neighbor? The key to Jesus' parable is the word "compassion."

The priest and Levite, who were bound by their pastoral calling to care for the scattered and bruised sheep ignored the wounded man and passed by on the other side. The Samaritan, who would be thought to have no responsibilities toward a wounded Israelite in a dangerous desert, treated the wounded man as though he were his own brother—ministering, nursing, paying all the costs in time, care and money.

The difference is dramatically pivoted on one word: "compassion." The priest and Levite saw and passed by. The Samaritan saw, had *compassion* and drew nigh.

The love that fulfills God's law is love like God's love. Jesus teaches that our righteousness must exceed the righteousness of the scribes and the Pharisees — not by more elaborate punctiliousness, but by another measure: the model of the Father's love. This means not only the benevolence of God's goodness who sends his rain on the just and the unjust. It means the mysterious grace of God's mercy in giving his only Son to die for sinners. Jesus' enemies called him a Samaritan, but it was he who was the true Shepherd of Israel. Unlike the false shepherds who did not care for the flock, Jesus is the true Shepherd who gives his life for the sheep. The compassion of kingdom love is the compassion of Jesus Christ, the compassion of God the Father.

What a model for love! God's grace is love that cannot be demanded and the love that God's law demands is love that cannot be demanded by any other law! The love of compassion is seeking love, missionary love, love that seeks the lost.

To the parable of the Good Samaritan we may join the parable of the prodigal son. Again the point of the parable is grace — the grace of the father's welcome springing from his love for his wayward son. The prodigal is presented as unworthy of that love. With his own lips he confesses that he is no more worthy to be called his father's son. It is enough that he should be permitted to work and eat as a hired servant. But the joy of the father's love heaps upon the prodigal the favors of sonship and welcomes him to a feast.

Just as the Pharisaical leaders are imaged in the priest and Levite of the other parable, so in this they are pictured in the figure of the older brother. He will not defile himself by coming in to his father's feast with a son who has wasted his inheritance with harlots. The inheritance has been divided and now he lays claim to all that remains: every robe, every ring, every pair of sandals, and especially every fatted calf!

But in outer darkness the father yet pleads with him to come in and share the feast of joy for a brother that was dead and is alive, was lost and is found.

By pointing to the Pharisees, Jesus indirectly reveals himself. He tells the parable in response to the criticism they have leveled at him for going in to eat with publicans and sinners. But Jesus, the true older brother, does not withdraw himself from sinners. Only to him may the Father say, "Son, thou art ever with me, and all that I have is thine" (Luke 15:31). But the true Heir freely shares his inheritance with sinners. More than that, he goes to seek sinners. Who can miss the figure of Jesus in the first parable of Luke 15? Jesus is the seeking Shepherd who calls his friends and neighbors to the feast of celebration. The figure of Jesus also stands in the shadow in the parable of the prodigal son. Were God's "First-born" like the Pharisees, sinners would not be sought or found. But Jesus seeks sinners, finds them in the pig-pen and brings them home. He not only shares heaven's feast with them — he spreads heaven's feast for them, for the bread and the cup by which guilty sinners are brought to God's feast are the broken body and shed blood of the Savior.

Jesus is the Son who knows and shares the joy of his Father's heart over one sinner who repents. He is the true older brother; his mission to the far country to seek and to save the lost is the mission of the Father's love. The demand of the parable is inescapable. The Pharisees stand condemned. Like the false older brother they do not seek the lost and they criticize Jesus for doing so. But what is the attitude of those who, like Jesus the true older brother, understand the Father's heart of compassion and share his joy over one sinner that repents? Those who know the meaning of grace will not only join in the feast for sinners, they will join in the search for sinners. Mission is demanded by Jesus' revelation of the love of the Father for sinners. The way of the kingdom Christ reveals is the path of seeking love.

The Kingdom of God the Power of Missions

The glory of God, the grace of God, the kingdom of God—in the New

Testament these themes are interwoven in the fabric of the gospel. The biblical concept of the kingdom centers upon the divine King. As the term *basileia* is used in the Gospels it has an active force: it means the *rule* of God rather than the *realm* of God. For example, we read of the Son of Man "coming in his kingdom" in a context that speaks of his coming in the glory of his Father with his angels (Luke 16:27, 28). "Coming in his kingdom" means coming in his royal power; it describes his dominion rather than his domain. Jewish nationalism had appropriated the Old Testament promises as a divine charter for the kingdom of Israel; Jesus restored the theocentric meaning of Old Testament eschatology by proclaiming the kingdom of *God*.

The whole history of salvation in the Old Testament declares that salvation is of the Lord. Ernst Bloch, the Marxist philosopher of the future, canonizes the category of the "possible" to quicken human hope. But reveals Himself as the God of the "impossible." Again and again the situation of the people of God becomes so desperate that deliverance is no longer possible. It is then that God saves — when Israel is in helpless slavery in Egypt, or pinned against the Red Sea by the chariots of Pharaoh, or crushed by the Midianites in the land of the promise. Indeed, God's great promises of the future are set against Ezekiel's vision of Israel in captivity — dead, dry bones filling the valley.

are impossibly good. Isaac is named "Laughter" to memorialize God's ridiculous promise to the aged Abraham and Sarah (Gen. 21:6, 7). Hidden designs of mercy too great for man to imagine are treasured up in God's promises (Jer. 33:3). In the last restoration God will give his people new hearts (Ezek. 36:26; 37:14). The Spirit of God breathes resurrection power upon the death valley of Israel's lost hopes. So impossible is man's sin that only God can be the Savior; so great are God's promises that he can keep them only by coming himself. The great triumphant chorus of Old Testament prophecy witnesses to the coming of the Lord: "Prepare ye in the desert a highway for our God!" (Isa. 40:3).

As God came down at Sinai to bear his people on eagle's wings to himself, so God will come down again in a second Exodus, but in so personal and full a way that even Sinai will be but a shadow and a foretaste. The impossibility of God's promise becomes divine reality when the virgin Mary bears her Son. "No word is impossible for God!" (Luke 1:37; Gen. 18:14).

God's royal saving power comes with the coming of his Son. By his words and deeds he manifests the power of the kingdom, indeed, his own power as Lord and King. The focus of the kingdom in the person and work of the King is the heart of the gospel.

Mission theology is kingdom theology; but kingdom as defined by the person, the work, the calling, of the King. Christ's kingship and the program of his kingdom are foolishness to the kingdoms of this world just as their Babel-building is fully before the King at God's right hand.

First, Christ's royal victory is final and ultimate and therefore *spiritual*. He would not lead a Jewish war of liberation against the Romans but he went alone to the cross to conquer Satan — by *dying* on the cross! Christ's final victory is radically spiritual. Judged by worldly standards the cross is Satan's victory and Christ's defeat. But in reality Satan is crushed by the atoning death of God's Son.

Second, Christ's victory calls his people to *suffer*. His program of salvation does not bring in the final judgment at once. This delay of judgment confused John the Baptist. John questioned Christ's identity as the Coming One precisely because his miracles seemed to inaugurate the blessings of the kingdom without bringing in the judgment of the kingdom. If Christ could raise the dead, why did he not deliver his own forerunner from Herod's prison? Jesus' reply to John is a strong assertion of his Lordship. "Blessed is he, whosoever shall find no occasion of stumbling in me" (Luke 7:23). John must trust Jesus to bring in his kingdom according to his own program. During the time that the final judgment is withheld, Jesus goes to the cross to bear the judgment so that those who deserve eternal judgment might have eternal life.

Christ is victorious. He has ascended and now rules in the power of his kingdom. The purposes of his kingdom are fulfilled on earth as men are brought back from darkness to become sons of light. Yet Christ will come again and after the judgment will form a new earth where perfect righteousness will be joined to perfect blessedness.

Missions requires us to understand the present and the future of Christ's kingdom design. Because Christ not only brings salvation but *is* salvation we may never conceive of salvation apart from the relation of persons to him. Liberation cannot define salvation, for biblical salvation does not consist in what we are delivered *from* but in whom we are delivered *to* ("on eagle's wings unto myself"). In uniting us to himself Christ does not promise that we will be delivered from suffering in this life. To the contrary, he calls us to his fellowship of suffering. Neither does Christ call us to bear the sword to bring in his kingdom by executing judgment in his name. The day of judgment will come soon enough, and God will avenge every injustice and judge every transgression.

Yet through suffering and forebearing, we wait for God's judgment; we do not enforce our own. We nevertheless participate in Christ's spiritual triumph — not by weapons of the flesh but by those spiritual weapons that are mighty before God to the casting down of strongholds and everything that is exalted against Christ (II Cor. 10:4-6).

Church growth is kingdom growth by the power of the Holy Spirit, the life of the New Creation. It cannot be achieved by human eloquence, wisdom, or power. Yet because the power is God's and not man's no human enterprise can compare with its effectiveness. The advocates of church growth have rightly recognized that the secularizing of the gospel in the theology of liberation changes the meaning of salvation and thereby destroys the gospel. That insight needs to be renewed and deepened. The theology of secular hope has been set before the church ever since Satan offered Jesus the kingdoms of this world without the cross. But the dynamic of biblical church growth flows from the nature of Christ's kingdom and here we all have much to learn before we really understand the Great Commission.

Not only does the kingdom center our attention on the King whose power brings the kingdom. It also forces us to consider the community of those brought into the kingdom by the power of the King.

Church Growth writers have often reminded us of the bonds of human community, warning against ignoring these ties as we would claim men and women for the kingdom. The apostle Paul was sensitive to the customs and cultures of Jews and Greeks; he was willing to conform to these traditions, to bring himself in bondage to them, as he says (I Cor. 9:19, 22), in order that he might win those who followed them. But Paul's own position was one of freedom; his voluntary conformity did not represent abandonment of his liberty in Christ, only a willingness to serve Christ in the gospel (v. 23). The liberty in which Paul serves is the liberty of a citizen of heaven, a new creature in Christ Jesus.

The gospel brings men into that liberty and forges a new fellowship, the fellowship of the Spirit-filled people of God. Again the key to our understanding is in Jesus Christ himself. The true circumcision are the people who worship by the Spirit of God, glory in Christ Jesus and have no confidence in the flesh (Phil. 3:3). The ties that join those born of the Spirit to Jesus Christ free them from the *dominion* of any earthly structure. Christians conform to social structures for the Lord's sake, but that very qualification is the sign of their deepest freedom.

The Christian's ultimate loyalty belongs to Jesus Christ alone. He is not a nationalist of an earthly state who finds in Christ the religious resources to enable him to fulfill his calling as a political being. He is a citizen of the heavenly polis who sustains his civic responsibilities here as a stranger and an alien; he has here no abiding city but seeks after that which is to come (Heb. 13:14). Even in the Reformed churches we have lost the identifying consciousness of the people of God found in the New Testament. The church is the circumcision, the true Israel of God. The whole controversy over the circumcision of the Gentiles presupposes this. Many Gentiles were God-fearers, attached to the synagogues but not members of the people of God through circumcision. If the gospel had aimed only at calling Gentiles to faith as Gentiles, no demand for circumcision would have been made. But both Paul and his Jewish-Christian opponents knew that Christian followers of the "Way" were not a new sect (Acts 24:5) but followers of the Way of the Lord, the God of the fathers (Acts 24:14). It was precisely because Gentiles were being admitted to the people of God that the Judaizers demanded that they be baptized.

To be sure, the people of God are renewed in Jesus Christ. But they are not thereby less but *more* of a community than was Israel of old. Because all are united to Christ, all "have fellowship with him in his graces, sufferings, death, resurrection, and glory: and being united to one another in love, they have communion in each other's gifts and graces, and are obliged to the performance of such duties, public and private, as do conduce to their mutual good, both in the inward and outward man."[4]

Through centuries of conflict the church has learned (we may hope!) the biblical lesson that the community of the people of God cannot be identified with the political state. But now the church must learn that it has an identity, a "theopolitical" form, the form of the community of Christ's kingdom in the world, a city set on a hill that cannot be hid.

Paul prays to the Father, from whom the whole family *(patria, "fatherdom")* in heaven and on earth is named, that all the saints may together comprehend the breadth, length, depth, and height of the fullness of Christ. Peter exhorts, "Love the brotherhood" (I Pet. 2:17). Those who were once aliens, strangers from the covenant and the commonwealth are now fellow-citizens with the Old Testament saints, members of the commonwealth, God's covenant people.

The form that the church takes cannot be an indifferent matter. The

---

[4]Westminster Confession of Faith XXVI: 1 (London: Blackwood & Sons, 1957), p. 40.

Holy Spirit who filled and fills the new people of God directed Christ's apostles as they established his assembly in the world. The New Testament provides form with freedom; among the "all things" of Christ's commandments to be taught to the nations is the pattern of fellowship in worship, edification, and witness that Christ has appointed for his people. Church growth is *church* growth —the building up in the world of the new people of God according to the word and will of the Spirit.

Here is an urgent concern. If our growing understanding of sociology outstrips our grasp of biblical theology, we may seek to build Christ's church from the wrong blueprints. Concretely, it is evident that in our efforts to respect sociological structures in evangelism we may unintentionally deny the biblical doctrines of the unity and catholicity of Christ's church. Christ's teachings are an offense to the mind of the natural man, and Christ's community is a rebuke to the tribalism, ethnocentricism, and prejudice of the world's social orders. The elder brother of the parable cannot be excused from the feast and provided with veal sandwiches to eat in the field with his friends. Pharisees who refuse to sit down to heaven's feast with publicans and sinners have no place in the kingdom of God.

Jesus predicts that the gospel will divide men, cutting between husband and wife, parent and child, brother and sister. More than that, Christ demands of everyone who follows him that he write off in advance every other tie: "If any man cometh unto me, and hateth not his own father, and mother, and wife and children, and brethren and sisters, yea and his own life also, he cannot be my disciple (Luke 14:26).

The exclusive bonds that unite us to Christ bind us together in the body of Christ. The unity of that fellowship must be proclaimed as part of the gospel and manifested if the church is to be presented as a pure virgin to Christ. The point at which human barriers are surmounted is the point at which a believer is joined to Christ and to his people. The sacrament of baptism does not seal the union of the believer with Paul, Cephas, or Apollos but with Christ. Christ is not divided and we cannot sanctify in his name the social barriers that wall up the Babylons of human pride.

The church can be a city set on a hill that cannot be hid only as it manifests in its life before the world the transforming reality of the community of the Holy Spirit. The church reaches out to every strata and segment of human societies: Peter is called as an apostle to the Jews and Paul to the Gentiles. But if Peter breaks church fellowship to accommodate himself to Jewish prejudice, he must receive deserved rebuke (Gal. 2:14). If the life of the new community is divided by the barriers of the old, the power of the gospel and of the kingdom of Christ is denied.

The Word of God the Message of Missions

"Scriptura Sola" was the watchword of the Reformation. The Word of God, drawn out of the rusty sheath of human traditions, pierced men's hearts. It quickened the church and reached forth to renew the nations.

So totally does the book of Acts join the growth of the church with the preaching of the Word of God that church growth is described as the growing and multiplying of the Word of God (Acts 6:7; 12:24; 19:20). Paul speaks of his missionary ministry as *fulfilling* the Word of God (Col. 1:25; Rom. 15:19). In this connection he reflects on the fulfillment of scriptural revelation in Jesus Christ (Col. 1:26f; Rom. 16:25-26). Paul preaches the mystery of Christ to the Gentiles and participates in the fulfillment of the promise that the Gentiles will hear and believe (Rom. 15:16). Moreover he fulfills the gospel by his rich ministry of the Word, proclaiming, admonishing, teaching, with the goal of presenting every man perfect in Christ (Col. 1:28). The spiritual comprehensiveness of that objective is matched by the geographical scope of Paul's ministry of fulfillment. Scorning to preach Christ where he has already been named, the great apostle serves the cosmic significance of the gospel by proclaiming it from Jerusalem to Illyricum and then pressing on to Spain that the Word may run to the ends of the earth (Rom. 15:19, 24).

Paul's sense of fulfilling the gospel discerns the basic and necessary relation between the message of salvation and the mission of proclaiming and teaching the Word to the ends of the earth. Both sides of this connection need new appreciation. The gosepl *is* a missionary message, not simply in the sense that it meets the needs of all men for salvation but in the fuller sense that the revelation of Jesus Christ fulfills God's purpose for the world. Christ is Lord of heaven and earth and all the nations are called to sing the praises of his name. When this scope of fulfillment is lost from view the message is no longer the rich message Paul preached. On the other hand, when the message is carried to the ends of the earth its depth as the Word of God must be preached. Paul labors according to God's working in him to present every man perfect in Christ, to teach the richness of Christ as the wisdom of God.

If the richness of the "fulfillment" gospel drives the church to the whole world, it is also true that the church in the whole world must have the richness of the fulfillment gospel. We sometimes assume that the Reformed church is guarding all the fullness of God's truth like the mythical dragon coiled around its treasure in a cave. The evangelical church, on the other hand, we see traveling far and wide with no more to distribute than four spiritual laws. But Paul's goal of fulfilling the gospel does much more than add zealous propagation to zealous preservation. It transforms both. When the Reformed church coils upon itself in the dragon posture it loses more than the missionary dynamic of the gospel. It loses in significant measure the gospel itself. In the gospel Christ lays claim to the nations. The gospel of the kingdom is his title to the promised land that must be possessed — God's inheritance of the nations. In analagous fashion when the evangelical church reduces the gospel to a facile formula for personal happiness it loses more than the glory of the wisdom of Christ. It loses in significant measure the very missionary dynamic that it seeks to serve. What is more, it loses the fullness that world-wide message must possess. A superficial gospel, because it is uprooted from the context of Scripture, it readily acquires a new context in the subculture of the evangelist. What is then preached, however passionately, is heard with a curious and unexpected difference in the cultural framework of the society where the missionary labors.

God's revelation in Jesus Christ is given in the context God himself has established in the history of his revelation and redemption. Scripture is not a human response to God's revelation, conditioned by the accidents of the culture in which the response is made. Rather, Scripture is God's Word, God's witness, God's revelation concerning his Son. God speaks from Sinai in a particular human language; God gives his words to Moses and the prophets; at last God speaks in his Son. Because God is the Lord of creation and history he is not compelled to make use of linguistic structures or cultural forms that are inappropriate to his purpose. Through the whole range of the history of salvation God uses tools that he has prepared for his own hand. By his own saving deeds and by his own chosen words he established the pattern of revelation, a pattern that is self-interpreting as well as self-authenticating. God's revelation is not to be interpreted by hermeneutical standards of our devising; rather it is God's revelation that is the standard and touchstone for all truth. The Bible, of course, does not contain all of God's revelation; God is revealed in all his works of creation and providence. But the Bible is unique as the permanent form of God's verbal revelation. God reveals and interprets his own plan of salvation in Jesus Christ. The mystery of God's speaking in human language is joined to the climactic mystery of God's coming in human flesh. God's revelation affirms the reality of meaning for man created in his image. God's speaking attests the validity of verbal communication; the miracle of Pentecost is God's sign that his message may be proclaimed and heard in every language under heaven. The very fact that the fulfillment of the prophecies given in Hebrew is declared in Greek shows us that there is not only one holy language. Not only does God choose and use those cultural forms that his providence has prepared, but his use of cultural patterns is grounded in the source and presupposition of all culture — that God created man in his own image. The Islamic doctrine that the Koran is untranslatable no doubt reflects Mohammed's contacts with Jewish and Christian beliefs about Scripture, but it presents a different understanding of the significance of inspiration, and, indeed of the relation of the Creator to his human creatures.

According to the revelation of the Bible the God who speaks addresses himself to all the nations. As has often been pointed out, the table of the nations in Genesis 10 precedes the call of Abraham in Genesis 12. God's purpose is to assemble his church from every tribe and tongue and people and nation (Rev. 7:9).

Yet the fact that the gospel may be preached in every language under heaven does not mean that it undergoes transformation in translation so that each culture produces its own gospel as it assimilates the stimulus of Christian preaching. Such transformations may occur, of course — witness the "gospel" of the Boxer rebellion, the tribal gospels of the Bantu sects, or, for that matter, the secularized "gospel" of American nationalism. But the fullness and concreteness of God's revelation in Scripture is the divine remedy for all such distortions. God does not enter history in a dimensionless point. Christ is not the abstract symbol of the infinite in the finite, a symbol that may be appropriated and contextualized in a thousand varieties of religious thought and experience. No, Christ comes to speak and act in perfectly definite ways and he comes to fulfill the promises of God given in the course of God's saving work on behalf of his people Israel. The meaning of the gospel is established in the total context of the history of redemption and revelation that the Bible presents. Given the biblical context, the gospel has the power to confront and transform cultures rather than to be transformed by them.

God's Word works this transformation as it is preached, and preaching must include the application of Scripture to the situation of those who hear it. Such application must be made to the structures of men's thoughts as well as to the patterns of their lives. In this sense a "contextual" theology arises in each distinct culture. Even though the gospel restructures the questions a culture asks it does nevertheless respond to them. A theologian has a double task: he must first subject himself utterly to the Word of God to perceive its structure as well as its teaching; he must also proclaim the teaching of Scripture to the world in which he lives. To do that effectively he must understand the men he would teach as well as the Bible he would teach. Of course, as he struggles to apply the Scriptures to men's questions and assumptions, to their errors, confusions, and insights, the theologian perceives unexpected facets of God's truth, facets that have significance not only in the context of his investigation but for all who would explore the richness of God's Word. Further, the missionary theologian who has God-given opportunities to display the treasures of God's revelation in more than one cultural setting will find new doors of understanding opened. He will be chastened by discovering how he has unthinkingly accommodated God's truth to his own cultural assumptions. He will also be amazed by the sufficiency of God's Word, and he will understand better how the gospel is fulfilled as it is carried to all the nations.

For this task the richness and fullness of God's Word must be the resource as well as the goal of the interpreter. The emphasis of Reformed theology on this fullness should mark Reformed theology as mission theology. The time is long past when mission leaders should set aside biblical theology to deal with more practical concerns. In the mission of the world-wide church of Christ no need is more immediate or practical than the need for biblical theology. Reformed theologians surely cannot afford to be patronizing toward brethren whose missionary zeal so honors the commandment of the Lord. But they should discern a new day of service and labor as they share with the people of God in every land what they have perceived of the glory of Christ in the gospel.

The glory of God, the grace of God, the kingdom of God, the Word of God — these are the great themes of Reformed theology, and these are the themes that must be central for the theology of missions. This is not strange, of course, for Reformed theology did rightly perceive the central themes of scripture, and the theology of Scripture is missionary theology, for the Son of Man came to seek and to save that which was lost. All the themes of scriptural theology center upon the Lord the Savior; in the confusion of the contemporary world and the crisis of the world mission of the church biblical theology brings us to the Lord himself: "This is my Son, my chosen: hear ye him" (Luke 9:35).

Selected Bibliography

General Bibliography

Alvin Martin, editor, *The Means of World Evangelization: Missiological Education at the Fuller School of World Mission*. South Pasadena: William Carey Library, 1974, pp. 261-332.

J. Robertson McQuilkin, *How Biblical is the Church Growth Movement?* Chicago: Moody Press, 1973, pp. 65-99.

Alan R. Tippett, editor, *God, Man and Church Growth*. Grand Rapids: William B. Eerdmans Publishing Company, 1973, pp. 43-46.

C. Peter Wagner, *Stop the World, I Want to Get On*. Glendale: Regal Books Division, G/L Publications, 1974, pp. 115-130.

General Materials

Roland Allen, *The Spontaneous Expansion of the Church*. Grand Rapids: William B. Eerdmans Publishing Company, 1962.

J. H. Bavinck, *An Introduction to the Science of Missions*. Philadelphia: The Presbyterian and Reformed Publishing Company, 1960.

R. Pierce Beaver, *From Missions to Mission*. New York: Association Press, 1964.

Peter Beyerhaus, "The Three Selves Formula: Is It Built on Biblical Foundations?" *International Review of Missions,* Vol. 53 (October, 1964).

_____, and Henry Lefever, *The Responsible Church and the Foreign Mission*. Grand Rapids: William B. Eerdmans Publishing Company, 1964.

Johannes Blauw, *The Missionary Nature of the Church*. New York: McGraw-Hill Book Company, Inc., 1962.

Harry Boer, *Pentecost and Missions*. Grand Rapids: William B. Eerdmans Publishing Company, 1961.

Malcolm Bradshaw, *Church Growth Through Evangelism in Depth*. South Pasadena: William Carey Library, 1968.

Edmund P. Clowney, *Called To the Ministry*. Philadelphia: Westminster Theological Seminary, 1964.

_____, *The Doctrine of the Church*. Philadelphia: Presbyterian and Reformed Publishing Company, 1969.

Orlando Costas, *The Church And Its Mission: A Shattering Critique From the Third World*. Wheaton: Tyndale House, 1974.

Richard R. DeRidder, *The Dispersion of the People of God*. Kampen: J. H. Kok, 1971.

J. D. Douglas, editor, *Let the Earth Hear His Voice*. Minneapolis: World Wide Publications, 1975.

Leighton Ford, *The Christian Persuader*. New York: Harper and Row, 1966.

Vergil Gerber, editor, *Missions in Creative Tension*. South Pasadena: William Carey Library, 1971.

_____, *God's Way to Keep a Church Going and Growing*. Glendale: Regal Books Division, G/L Publications, 1973.

Arthur Glasser, "Putting Theology to Work," *Theology News and Notes,* Vol. XVI, No. 2 (June, 1972).

_____, "Church Growth Theology," *Church Growth Movement. Proceedings. Eleventh Biennial Meeting, Association of Professors of Missions*. Nashville, Tenn.: Association of Professors of Missions, June 12-14, 1972.

Norman Goodall, editor, *Missions Under the Cross*. London: Edinburgh House Press, 1953.

Michael Green, *Evangelism in the Early Church*. London: Hodder and Stoughton, 1970.

Gerhard Hoffmann, "Considerations on Integration of Church and Mission in Germany," *International Review of Mission,* Vol. 58 (July, 1969).

Herbert C. Jackson, "Some Old Patterns for New in Missions," *Occasional Bulletin of the Missionary Research Library,* Vol. 12, No. 10 (December, 1961).

Edwin Jacques, "An Equal Partnership Structure," *Evangelical Missions Quarterly,* Vol. 9, No. 2 (1973).

R. B. Kuiper, *God-Centered Evangelism.* Grand Rapids: Baker Book House, 1963.

Donald McGavran, *The Bridges of God.* New York: Friendship Press, 1955.

_____, *How Churches Grow.* London: World Dominion Press, 1959.

_____, editor, *Church Growth and Christian Mission.* New York: Harper and Row, 1965.

_____, *Understanding Church Growth.* Grand Rapids: William B. Eerdmans Publishing Company, 1970.

Donald McGavran, editor, *Eye of the Storm.* Waco, Texas: Word Books, 1972.

_____, editor, *Crucial Issues in Missions Tomorrow.* Chicago: Moody Press, 1972.

_____, with Win C. Arn, *How To Grow A Church.* Glendale: Regal Books Division, G/L Publications, 1973.

Robert Martin-Achard, *A Light to the Nations.* Edinburgh: Oliver and Boyd, 1962.

Daniel T. Miles, *Upon the Earth. The Mission of God and the Missionary Enterprise of the Churches.* New York: McGraw-Hill Book Company, Inc., 1962.

Stephen Neill, *History of Christian Missions.* Grand Rapids: William B. Eerdmans Publishing Company, 1964.

_____, Gerald H. Anderson, John Goodwin, editors, *Concise Dictionary of the Christian World Mission.* Nashville: Abingdon Press, 1971.

O. Guy Oliver, *Church Growth and Reformed Theology.* Jackson: Mimeographed privately by Reformed Theological Seminary, 1973.

James I. Packer, *Evangelism and the Sovereignty of God.* London: Inter-Varsity Fellowship, 1961.

George Peters, *A Biblical Theology of Missions.* Chicago: Moody Press, 1972.

J. Waskom Pickett, *Christ's Way to India's Heart.* Lucknow: W. W. Bell, 1960.

_____, *Christian Mass Movements in India.* New York: Abingdon Press, 1933.

_____, A. L. Warnshuis, G. H. Singh, D. A. McGavran, *Church Growth and Group Conversion.* Pasadena: William Carey Library, 1962.

_____, *The Dynamics of Church Growth.* New York: Abingdon Press, 1963.

Sidney Rooy, "The Concept of Man in the Missiology of Donald McGavran: A Model of Anglosaxon Missiology in Latin America," *Westminster Theological Journal,* Vol. XXXVII. No. 2 (Winter, 1975).

James Scherer, *Missionary, Go Home!* Englewood Cliffs, N. J.: Prentice-Hall, 1964.

Wilbert R. Shenk, editor, *The Challenge of Church Growth.* Elkhart, In.: Institute of Mennonite Studies, 1973.

Alan R. Tippett, *Verdict Theology in Missionary Theory.* Lincoln, III.: Lincoln Christian College Press, 1969.

_____, *Church Growth and the Word of God.* Grand Rapids: William B. Eerdmans Publishing Company, 1970.

Walter Vogels, "Covenant and Universalism," *Zeitschrift fur Missionswissenschaft und Religionswissenschaft,* Vol. 57. Part 1 (January, 1973)

C. Peter Wagner, Editor, *Church/Mission Tensions Today*. Chicago: Moody Press, 1972.

_____, *Frontiers in Missionary Strategy*. Chicago: Moody Press, 1971.

B. B. Warfield, "Are They Few That Be Saved?" *Biblical and Theological Studies*. Philadelphia: The Presbyterian and Reformed Publishing Company, 1962.

Ralph Winter, *The Twenty-Five Unbelievable Years, 1945-1969*. South Pasadena: William Carey Library, 1970.

_____, and R. Pierce Beaver, *The Warp and the Woof*. South Pasadena: William Carey Library, 1971.

Tetsunao Yamamori and E. LeRoy Lawson, *Introducing Church Growth*, Cincinatti, Ohio: Standard Publishing Company, 1975.